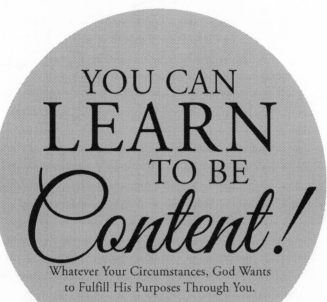

YOU CAN LEARN TO BE *Content!*

Whatever Your Circumstances, God Wants to Fulfill His Purposes Through You.

SARAH O. MADDOX

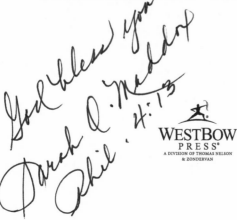

God bless you
Sarah O. Maddox
Phil. 4:13

WESTBOW
PRESS®
A DIVISION OF THOMAS NELSON
& ZONDERVAN

Unless otherwised indicated, scripture taken from the New King James Version. Copyright © 1979, 1980, 1982 by Thomas Nelson, Inc. Used by permission. All rights reserved.

Taken from My Utmost for His Highest® by Oswald Chambers, edited by James Reimann, © 1992 by Oswald Chambers Publications Assn., Ltd., and used by permission of Discovery House, Grand Rapids MI 49501. All rights reserved.

"He is Here," Words and Music by Kirk Talley, Kirk Talley Music, 1988. Used by Permission.

Author Credits: Six Published Books

WestBow Press books may be ordered through booksellers or by contacting:

WestBow Press
A Division of Thomas Nelson & Zondervan
1663 Liberty Drive
Bloomington, IN 47403
www.westbowpress.com
1 (866) 928-1240

Because of the dynamic nature of the Internet, any web addresses or links contained in this book may have changed since publication and may no longer be valid. The views expressed in this work are solely those of the author and do not necessarily reflect the views of the publisher, and the publisher hereby disclaims any responsibility for them.

Any people depicted in stock imagery provided by Thinkstock are models, and such images are being used for illustrative purposes only. Certain stock imagery © Thinkstock.

ISBN: 978-1-5127-2766-1 (sc)
ISBN: 978-1-5127-2767-8 (hc)
ISBN: 978-1-5127-2765-4 (e)

Library of Congress Control Number: 2016901051

Print information available on the last page.

WestBow Press rev. date: 03/29/2016

Contents

Dedication

I lovingly dedicate this book to my precious granddaughters:

Chelsea Elizabeth Maddox

Emily Kendall Redd

Anna Catherine Maddox

You three girls have brought great joy to my life!

Philippians 4: 11b-13: "... for I have learned to be content, whatever the circumstances may be. I know now how to live when things are difficult and I know how to live when things are prosperous. In general and in particular I have learned the secret of facing either poverty or plenty. I am ready for anything through the strength of the one who lives within me" (J.B. Phillips New Testament).

Preface

This book highlights my life's journey of seeking to be content wherever I have lived. As was true for the Apostle Paul, it has been a learning experience for me. Paul states in Philippians 4:11b, "I have learned to be content, whatever the circumstances may be."[1] I am grateful for God's patience and forbearance when so often I have been a slow learner.

My pilgrimage has never been boring; it has been filled with frequent detours and bumps in the road. The disruptive moments in my life have provided new challenges year after year. God's prompting to put a wreath on the front door of one of our houses was the inspiration for this book. That wreath symbolized acceptance of the home He had given us; it was my first step in learning to be content in that location. I pray that some of the experiences I share will help you in *your* life's journey, as you, too, seek to be the contented woman God desires.

I am still learning lessons about contentment. None of us ever "arrives." No matter how long you have been a Christian (and

I have been one for several decades), as you study God's Word and listen to His voice, you will learn new things day after day. Romans 15:13 states, "Now may the God of hope fill you with all joy and peace in believing, that you may abound in hope by the power of the Holy Spirit." Regardless of your circumstances, I pray that God will fill you with hope and encourage you to keep on keeping on. Always remember that our God is the "Blessed Controller" of all things.[2]

Acknowledgements

I want to express my deep appreciation to Francis A. McDaniel for allowing me to include her beautiful poetry in this book. You will be uplifted and blessed by her inspiring poems, all of which are based on Scripture. I am truly grateful to Fran McDaniel, Kelly Beach, and Jana Chapman for their labor of love in editing my book. Their insights and suggestions have been priceless!

Thank you, Gwen Ash, for working tirelessly with me, answering questions and guiding me in the publication process. Your help has been invaluable. I also wish to express my gratitude to every person at Westbow Press who has had a part in seeing that my book was published. For all the hours you have spent on my behalf, thank you so much.

To my wonderful husband Roland, I say thank you for everything you have done for me and experienced with me as I was writing and publishing this book. To have been married more than fifty years is a marvelous blessing; to be married to you has been the greatest blessing of my life! To God be the glory!

--Sarah O. Maddox

CHAPTER 1

A Life-Changing Experience

But godliness with contentment is great
gain – 1Timothy 6:6 (HCSB)

Acceptance

Have you noticed how many homes have wreaths on their front doors? Observing the diverse wreaths women choose has been a delightful adventure for me. The size of the house does not determine the beauty of the wreath. Some of the largest homes I've viewed do not have wreaths on their front doors. Yet I know of a little cottage on a back road in the mountains of East Tennessee that always displays an attractive wreath to match the season.

I'm not certain who first suggested that I put a wreath on our front door. While my husband was building a new home for us in Memphis, Tennessee, we often drove out to check the progress. On the way to our subdivision, we passed multiple houses with wreaths on their front doors. I was inspired to do the same.

When we moved into our new home, I could hardly wait to hang wreaths on our doors – yes, *doors*. Since our new house had two front doors, one wreath would not suffice. To lessen the expense of decorating two wreaths, I had to be very creative. That signaled a small problem – handmade creations were not my specialty! *What should I do?* The answer: *copy what others did!*

Off to the craft store I drove, hoping to find matching green wreaths, a variety of flowers and eye-catching ribbon to complement the color of our doors. When I returned home with my purchases, I decorated the wreaths using a glue gun and that little green wire I learned to love – it had so many uses. My goal was to have something that looked attractive from the street and not too shabby up close.

My wreaths were never perfect – perhaps they didn't look store bought – but they served my purpose. To me, the wreaths conveyed a message: "A family now lives in this house. You are welcome to come for a visit." We lived in that home for twenty-four years, from our children's preschool days until several years beyond their graduation from high school. We were all very content living there. Year after year, I changed the wreaths to correspond with the seasons. Needless to say, by the time we moved, I had a substantial collection of wreaths!

Putting wreaths on my doors was a practice I continued through the years until we moved into our sixth house which was in Nolensville, Tennessee. Moving, as we all know, is hectic! To complicate things, I had surgery in the midst of our move. I simply forgot to put a wreath on the front door! This new house was not my favorite. It was, however, the house the Lord had given us for this season of our lives. I needed to keep that fact in mind. That fact needed to sink into my psyche. A few months later, God saw to it that it did!

After I had recuperated from surgery, I began teaching a Bible study for young women entitled *Mother Wise*, an excellent Bible study written by Denise Glenn.[1] I was having a joyful time teaching it until we came to the lesson on contentment. Since the teacher is often tested on what she is teaching, it was my turn. Many times, as a part of the lesson, I used illustrations from my past. The following week, my illustration came from the previous weekend. Talk about fresh illustrations!

That weekend, a friend with a degree in interior design came to critique my house and give me suggestions for decorating. During lunch, we began to talk about the house *she* wanted to buy. Two of her most important considerations were its front elevation and the way in which the house sat on the lot.

That night I mulled over our visit. As I thought about the outside of our house and the way it was positioned on the sloping lot, I felt discontentment rising within me. The negatives about my house began to manifest their ugly heads. They reminded me, "You have never liked this brick. You would not have chosen it for a house you were building. You don't like the way the house sits on the lot, and Roland isn't a fan of corner lots." By the time the negative voices had stopped, I was an unhappy camper. But was the *house* the only cause of my discontentment? When I examined my heart, I knew the *location* was a factor, too; I did not want to live in that small town!

When I got into bed, my discontentment climbed in with me. My soul was in turmoil, knowing that God could not be pleased with my resistant spirit. I had not accepted this house or its location as a gift from God's hands. Until I yielded my situation to the Lord, sleep was out of the question. I quickly got out of bed and asked God's forgiveness for resisting His plans. God had brought us to this location for a reason. I must accept this house and town as my new place of ministry and learn to be content.

Suddenly, I sensed God's prompting to put a wreath on our front door. I had forgotten to put one there. I knew that a wreath would add warmth and friendliness to our home, thereby making it more appealing. It would also serve as a continual reminder to praise God for giving us this new home.

When I awoke the next morning, like a neon sign, the admonition flashed across my mind: "Put a wreath on the door." In our garage we still had boxes full of unpacked accessories; fortunately, I remembered which one contained my wreaths. I hurried out the back door to find a suitable wreath. When I opened the box, a pretty, but forgotten wreath greeted me. It was perfect for the front door. Gently lifting it out of the box, I carried it to the front hall. Finding my wreath holder in a nearby drawer, I opened the door and placed the wreath on it! For me, that wreath symbolized *acceptance* of God's provision for me. It was *my first step in learning to be content where God had placed me.*

I believe that every Christian has a purpose to fulfill while on this earth. It was not until that time of discontentment, however, that I began to understand why learning to be content is so important in fulfilling that purpose. As we learn to be content in "whatsoever state we are" (as Paul said),[2] we find the freedom to embrace the plans God has designed especially for us.

Our loving heavenly Father wants us to bring glory to His name in every season and every station of our lives. To do so, we must *accept* His plans and provisions, even when they aren't always the plans and provisions we had envisioned. He longs for us to surrender to

His perfect will, remembering that as Philippians 2: 13 says, "....it is God Who is at work within you, giving you the will and the power to achieve His purpose."[3] That familiar verse in Proverbs is so applicable to our lives: "Trust in the Lord with all your heart, and lean not on your own understanding. In all your ways acknowledge Him, and He shall direct your paths" (Proverbs 3: 5-6).

Perhaps you haven't thought about putting a wreath on your front door. I encourage you to consider this practice. An attractive wreath is cheerful and welcoming – a lifter of spirits on a gloomy day. Hopefully, it will encourage you to thank the Lord for the home He has provided for you. Since women choose many different types of attractive decorations for their front doors, I suggest that a wreath be displayed at least four times a year.

Having a wreath on your front door will have greater significance if you understand the symbolisms of the wreath (see Chapter 2). While your wreath may not symbolize the *acceptance* of God's provision, as mine did on Powder Springs Drive, acceptance of "whatever state you are in,"[4] is often the first step toward contentment. Whether or not we put wreaths on our doors, God wants us to learn to be content.

Acceptance of God's Provisions is a Part of Learning to Be Content.

"Acceptance is taking from God's hand absolutely anything He chooses to give us, looking into His face in love and trust – even in thanksgiving – and knowing that the confines of the hedges within which He has placed us are good, even perfect, however painful they may be simply because He Himself has given them." – Author Unknown [5]

Chapter 2

An Eye-Opening Walk

Don't neglect to show hospitality – Hebrews 13:2a (HCSB)

Southern hospitality has long been a hallmark of the states in which I have lived – Mississippi, Kentucky, and Tennessee. The pastor's home in which I grew up had an open door policy. Mother would come to the breakfast table fully dressed with her makeup perfect and her jewelry in place. She wanted to be ready for company, no matter how early someone might come to the preacher's house. Since I am not a morning person, I haven't quite followed her example of being dressed for the day when I come to the kitchen each morning. I have attempted, however, to welcome everyone who comes to our house with Southern hospitality!

My mother and mother-in-law were both gracious Southern ladies. For ten years, my mother-in- law, Lucille Maddox Johnson, lived in a lovely retirement facility in Clarksdale, Mississippi. Like many other similar residences, this complex had multiple halls. While visiting her one cold winter day, I decided to walk indoors for exercise. As I strolled down the halls, I noticed something extraordinary – a wreath or other flower arrangement adorned nearly every door. Like the residents who lived there, they were all different and unique.

As I continued my walk, thoughts paraded across my mind. I asked myself: *Why are all the doors decorated? Perhaps having a wreath on the door makes visitors aware that someone lives there. Maybe it is to let guests know that the lady who lives there cares about the entrance to her apartment – plain beige doors don't look inviting.* Wreaths are symbols of welcome, caring and hospitality. Flowers are meant to lift the spirits and express one's love. Seeing all those different styles and colors was a happy sight. I wanted to knock on each door and meet the person who lived in that apartment. If I saw an unadorned door, I felt an urge to buy a wreath for the door.

As I meandered down hall after hall, another question came to mind: *How was this tradition begun in the first place?* That thought necessitated a trip to my computer to look up the history of wreaths. What I found was quite interesting. One paragraph that really caught my attention explained the symbolism of the wreath. Surely I knew the symbolism earlier in my life, but that day it seemed like new information. The circular design of the wreath symbolizes immortality, everlasting life, the circle of family, and unending love. An evergreen wreath is the symbol of eternal life. (That is why many churches still have a Christmas service called "The Hanging of the Greens").[1]

After I learned the true symbolism of wreaths, displaying a wreath held deeper significance. Even if no one else knew, in my heart I knew: My wreath symbolized the everlasting life each member of our family received when Jesus became his or her Savior. It symbolized our family circle and the unending love that Jesus has for each one of us.[2] It also symbolized *my acceptance of what God had provided for us.* I believe that once a person is aware of its symbolism, putting a wreath on the door can be a very special practice. Shouldn't we teach this to our children and grandchildren?

Everlasting Life, the Family Circle, Unending Love, Immortality;[3] and for me, Accepting God's Provisions.

Take the Time to Reflect on the Symbolism of Wreaths.

10

CHAPTER 3

God's Waiting Room

Wait on the LORD; Be of good courage, And He shall strengthen your heart; Wait, I say, on the LORD – Psalm 27:14

Memphis, Tennessee, was our hometown for thirty-two years. In nineteen ninety, we moved into my dream home, courtesy of Roland and our son Alan, both of whom were home builders. Having lived in my previous house for twenty-four years, I was beginning to doubt that I would ever have the home for which I had dreamed and planned so long. My husband and son came through for me; I was thrilled with our new home. A friend gave me a lovely floral decoration for my front door; I placed it on the

Sarah O. Maddox

door with great anticipation of joyful times to come in this home of my dreams.

We had put down roots in Memphis and never expected to live anywhere else. We soon learned, however, that God had a different plan for us. In the spring of nineteen ninety-two, we were confronted with the possibility of a huge lifestyle change. An exciting position in Nashville was offered to my husband.

There were several compelling reasons for staying in Memphis: We had lived in our dream home for only eighteen months, barely long enough to get it decorated. This move would mean a career change for Roland at age fifty-five. We loved our dear friends and our wonderful church, and we were both actively involved in the community. Two very important events were to take place in Memphis that year – our daughter and daughter-in-law were to present us with grandbabies, three weeks apart. Leaving Memphis did not seem to be a logical idea. We were very content!

We began to pray earnestly, immediately setting aside a day to fast and pray. On that day, God led Roland to Genesis 12, Psalm 90:12, and Luke 14:26-27. In Genesis 12:1, God said to Abraham, "Get out of your country, from your family and from your father's house, to a land that I will show you." Psalm 90:12 advised, "So teach us to number our days, that we may gain a heart of wisdom." This verse in HCSB read, "Teach us to make our days count…"

12

Luke 14:27 plainly stated, "But whoever does not bear his cross and come after Me, cannot be my disciple."

Roland soon became convinced, like Abraham in Genesis, God was calling us to leave our land and our relatives to go to a land God had shown us –Nashville, Tennessee. I was wholeheartedly in agreement with him; God had spoken to my heart, too. We both believed that Roland had been called by God to LifeWay Christian Resources in Nashville.

Near the end of the summer of nineteen ninety-two, we moved to Middle Tennessee, renting an apartment in Brentwood, a suburb south of Nashville. For the next nine months, we diligently searched for a house. Having lived in our dream home in Memphis, the object of our search was a comparable house. There was just one problem…comparable homes in Brentwood were more expensive than Roland wanted to pay. It took several months to find the home God had for us.

Moving from a city in which we had lived for thirty-two years was not an easy adjustment. Our days in Memphis had been overflowing with family, friends and fellowship. Our pastor was one of the most outstanding in our denomination. Starting over was going to be especially difficult for me, a stay-at-home mom.

I knew very few residents of Brentwood. We attended a church forty-five minutes away. The apartment dwellers didn't carry on conversations other than to say hello in response to my greetings. Those first few weeks I could hardly wait for my husband to get home from work. Roland left home around six o'clock each morning before I was awake. He came home at four- thirty in the afternoon, sleepy and tired. During many of our conversations, his head would drop, and he would fall asleep. He had obviously used his word quotient for the day while I was just getting started!

Even though I was very lonely, I had perfect peace about our move. I knew beyond a shadow of a doubt that God had led us there, but learning to be content was going to take time! In God's perfect timing, the first year we lived in Brentwood, *LifeWay Press* produced an awesome Bible study entitled *Experiencing God.* I began to study it in my Quiet Time each day. God used that study to strengthen my faith and teach me important lessons. One morning I read this story:

> Dr. Henry Blackaby's Canadian church had started its first mission church. The mission church had called a man named Jack to be the mission pastor, but they had no money for his moving expenses or his salary. The members were praying earnestly for the needed funds.
>
> Dr. Blackaby says: "We had stepped out in faith believing that God wanted Jack to pastor our mission in Prince Albert. Except for a few people in California, I didn't know anybody who could help us financially. I began to ask myself, '*How in the world will God make this provision?*' Then it dawned on me that as long as God knew where I was, He could cause anybody in the world to know where

I was. As long as He knew our situation, He could place our need on the heart of anybody He chose."

Dr. Blackaby goes on to say, "Jack started his move of faith to Canada, convinced that God had called him. I then received a letter from a church in Fayetteville, Arkansas, that read: 'God has laid it on our heart to send one percent of our mission giving to Saskatchewan missions. We are sending a check ($1,100) to use however you choose.'"

When Jack arrived in Canada, he went to Henry's house. Henry met him in the driveway and asked, "Jack, what did it cost you to move?"

Jack answered, "Well, Henry, as best I can tell, it cost me $1,100."

Dr. Blackaby concludes: "We took a step of faith, believing that the God who knows where we are, is the God who can touch people anywhere and cause them to know where we are and what we need."[1]

After reading of the amazing way in which God met this church's needs, I fell to my knees in front of our fireplace. I cried out to my Heavenly Father, *Oh, God, do You know where I am?* (Of course, I knew He did). *I am so lonely. I know we are supposed to be here; there is no doubt in my mind about that. But Lord, I boldly come to Your Throne of Grace to find mercy and help for **my** needs!* (Hebrews 4:16)

God answered my prayer in His ways and His timing. I enrolled in the Brentwood Bible Study Fellowship, which gave me the opportunity to participate in a wonderful Bible study as well as to meet new Christian friends. We bought an incredible house, moving into it in July of 1993. One of my first tasks was to put a wreath on the door! (Of the eleven houses in which we have lived, this house is my all-time favorite.)

At our church in Memphis, I had the privilege of teaching Sunday School for over thirty years. I taught single women for the first half and young married women the last half. Teaching young women was my passion. After we had lived in our new home for a few months, I realized the ministry I missed the most was teaching the Bible to younger women.

I knelt and prayed, *Oh, Lord, I don't have to teach a large group of women. If it is Your will, could I have five ladies to teach?* In a few months, I started a Bible study in our home. The first morning we met, *five women* were there for the study. Praise the Lord!

Never did I dream it would take such a long time to learn to be content in Brentwood. I have always loved meeting new people. Brentwood was a marvelous place to live – everything about it was unique and special. Exciting activities filled my days. I shall ever be grateful to Clark Brittain for including me in so many of Nashville's Christian events. I must admit, however, that it took me five years to learn to be truly content. I realize now that God wanted me to learn to be content while in His Waiting Room. It was not His desire for me to be such a slow learner, but obviously, I was.

At the beginning of our sixth year in Brentwood, it dawned on me while driving home one day that I was very content! The following five years in Brentwood were awesome! God led us to a church nearby, where opportunities for ministry opened up almost immediately. In Sunday School Roland taught young adult men, and I taught their wives. I was asked to teach *The Joy of Living Bible Study*[2] to the moms in our church. During that time, God gave me wonderful Christian friends and led me to write books for Christian women. "The joy of the Lord was my strength" (Nehemiah 8: 10).

Near the end of our tenth year in Brentwood, I had to face the reality that Roland's ministry at LifeWay was coming to a close. We would be moving soon after he retired. I was not ready to leave! In the weeks before we moved, I praised the Lord over and over for the privilege of living there. I thanked Him for all the blessings He had bestowed. Learning to be content had taken much longer than I had anticipated, but by giving God time and following His directions, I had learned contentment!

How had I learned to be content? Through much Bible study and prayer. Those first years in Brentwood, I frequently claimed Isaiah 50:10, "Who among you fears the Lord, listening to the voice of His servant? Who among you walks in darkness, and has no light? Let him trust in the name of the Lord; let him lean on his God" (HCSB). Isaiah was speaking to those who feared the Lord and were waiting to hear from Him; unfortunately, they were receiving no "light" concerning the path they should choose – they were "walking in darkness." As they waited, Isaiah admonished them to trust in the name of the Lord and lean on God. While I was waiting on God for answers, I knew I must do the same – trust in the name of the Lord and hang on to my God. What a comfort to know He would never let go of me!

During our time in Middle Tennessee, God provided several speaking opportunities for me. In many of my messages, I highlighted this Isaiah verse. One day at the conclusion of a message, a lady came up to me and asked, "Have you read verse eleven?" Not remembering the verse, I read it on the way home from the event. Isaiah 50:11 says: "Look, all you who kindle a fire, who encircle yourself with firebrands; walk in the light of your fire and in the firebrands you have lit! This is what you'll get from My hand: you will lie down in a place of torment." This verse warns us not to take things into our own hands while we are waiting for God's answers. If we do, what will be the result? We will "lie down in a place of torment."

A second passage of Scripture on which I meditated contains a command, coupled with a promise. It is Hebrews 10: 36-38a:

> Do not cast away your confidence, which has great reward.
> For you have need of endurance,

so that after you have done the will of God,
you may receive the promise:
For yet a little while,
He who is coming will come,
And will not tarry.
Now the just shall live by faith.

God admonishes us not to "cast away our confidence" in Him. In God's Waiting Room, it is easy to move to a mindset of doubt and fear. My Biblical namesake, Sarah, took things into her

> In God's Waiting Room, it is easy to move to a mindset of doubt and fear.

own hands as she waited on God to answer. We are still reaping the results of Sarah and Abraham's unwillingness to trust God and wait for Him to fulfill His promises to them (see Genesis 16:1-6). Waiting on God to answer our prayers is not easy, but it is worth the wait. We need to live by faith, believing "what He has promised, He is able to perform" (Romans 4:21).

A third verse which gave me much hope was Isaiah 64:4: "From ancient times no one has heard, no one has listened, no eye has seen any God except You, who acts on behalf of the one who waits for Him" (HCSB). God was at work on my behalf, even when I couldn't *see* what He was doing! As 2 Corinthians 5: 7 instructs, I must "walk by faith and not by sight."

In his excellent book, *When God Doesn't Make Sense*, James Dobson writes:

> "If you find yourself on the dusty road to Emmaus today, and the circumstances in your life have left you confused and depressed, never assume God's silence or apparent inactivity is evidence of His disinterest. With God, even when nothing is happening, *something* is happening. The Lord is at work in His own unique way even when our prayers seem to echo back from an empty universe."[3]

Two of the previous Scripture passages list things we *should not do* in God's Waiting Room: Do *not* take things into your own hands and do *not* cast away your confidence in God. But there are five things I believe we *should be doing:* Give God time, pray without ceasing, study God's Word, claim His promises, and trust and obey. (See the Appendix, "What to Do While Waiting for God's Answers.")

Sometimes Learning to Be Content Takes Longer Than We Desire!

Beyond the Shadow

By Frances A. McDaniel

When Heaven is silent and waves of sorrow engulf your heart
Like billows unrelenting, they crash and rend your soul apart.
When the future looms foreboding like a mountain fortress high,
Look beyond the shadow valley to Christ Jesus drawing nigh.
Observe with spirit eyes illumined by His light and majesty;
Behold the Lamb, glorious Redeemer, enthroned in righteous
    sovereignty.
Abounding grace, all sufficient, enabling limitless supply
Will flood your soul with living water, the gift of God, on Him rely.

When hope seems an illusion of imagination gone awry,
Choose to will and worship singing, "My God, I'll trust You
    though I die."
Light divine and risen glory will pierce the darkness by design,
Perfect peace, transcendent Presence will guard your heart and
    intertwine.
Take up the cup of salvation, relinquish all to God alone,
Trust Christ to build His temple, He will complete what He's begun.
A minister of comfort He'll prove to be and make of you.
Trouble comes to serve His purpose, sovereign grace will see you
    through.

When heaven seems hushed and silent, remember you are not alone.

For standing in the shadows, the Father watches o'er His own.

Underneath you and sustaining are His everlasting arms;

Jehovah Jireh, faithful Provider in grace will shelter from all harm.

In the midst of fiery trials, God preserves and intervenes.

Walk by faith in prayer believing, rejoice in joy, on Jesus lean.

As the Spirit blows upon God's garden that His spices may flow out,

It's Christ in you, the hope of glory, beyond the shadow of a doubt.[4]

II Corinthians 1: 3-5; I Peter 1: 3-9, 4: 12-13;

Song of Solomon 4: 16

CHAPTER 4

Unmet Expectations

My soul, wait silently for God alone, for my
expectation is from Him – Psalm 62: 5

A young minister and his wife were heavily courted to join the ministerial staff of a growing church. The opportunity to serve on this church staff seemed perfect for them. As they prayed for God's will to be done, they felt His definite leading. After serving there for a few years, things began to deteriorate. They faced many unmet expectations. While they were waiting for the Lord to guide them as to whether to go or stay, the wife put a wreath on the door. She realized her joy, her peace, and her contentment did not come from people or circumstances – they came from the

Lord alone. The wreath was her way of saying that this was her home until the Lord showed them otherwise.

If we search for the root causes of our dissatisfaction and discontentment, we often find unmet and unrealistic expectations buried beneath our unhappiness. <u>Having unrealistic expectations of someone or something sets us up for major disappointments.</u> Unmet expectations can steal our joy, peace, and contentment if they are not viewed from God's perspective.

> Having unrealistic expectations of someone or something sets us up for major disappointments.

Yes, disappointments can arise when a person or thing does not live up to what we had expected.

> It may be that the house you are living in does *not* live up to your expectations.
> The church you attend has *not* lived up to your expectations.
> The person you thought was going to be your friend has proven *not* to be a true friend.
> Your job has *not* turned out like you thought it would.
> Your child is *not* meeting your expectations in his school work.
> And we won't bring up your spouse!

The late Gladys Hunt once coined what she called "The Five D's of Satan's Strategy: Disappointment, Doubt, Discouragement, Disillusionment, Despair."[1] I have added two to her list:

Discontentment
Defeat

A disappointment comes, and I get discouraged. Discouragement can lead to doubts about God's goodness and care. The next thing I know, I am disillusioned and no longer content with my circumstances. If I don't deal with my discontentment, I can find myself on a slippery slope, spiraling down from discontentment to defeat to despair. It is only as I depend on the Lord in every situation that I can learn to be content – only when I surrender my will to His perfect will, die to my own desires and embrace His. Only when I believe that He will supply my needs all the time, and trust Him to do so, will I be content. Philippians 4:19: says, "And My God shall supply all your needs according to His riches in glory by Christ Jesus" (HCSB). All my needs, all the time!

> It is only as I depend on the Lord in every situation that I can learn to be content

Over and over we read in God's Word that His grace is sufficient. It is sufficient for your needs; it is sufficient for mine. The Bible states in 2 Corinthians 9:8, "And God is able to make all grace abound toward you, that you, always having all sufficiency in all things, may have an abundance for every good work." I love this verse of assurance. Look at the words: *all, every, all grace, all things,* and an *abundance* for every good work. Has Paul missed anything in this verse? I don't believe so! I must yield my situation to God and *allow* Him to pour out His grace upon me.

There will always be friends who have more money than we do, and often they will have larger and finer houses than ours. Sometimes our children will disappoint us in unbelievable ways. And, heaven forbid, the husband you love may ask for a divorce. (Or your situation may be worse than we can imagine!) BUT GOD!

Years ago I discovered an old hymn that comforts me when I am seemingly at the end of my rope. It gives me the assurance that God's grace is more than sufficient. It is the hymn "He Giveth More Grace," written long ago by Annie Johnson Flint. There is a stanza that has comforted me from the time I first saw the lyrics. It says:

"When we have exhausted our store of endurance,
When our strength has failed, ere the day is half done,
When we reach the end of our hoarded resources,
Our Father's full giving has simply begun." [2]

Is it possible to *learn* to be content, whatever our circumstances? Matthew 19:26 declares, "With God, all things are possible."

In Mississippi, a few years ago, my mother introduced me to a dear friend of hers. She was a lovely Christian woman who was filled with the joy of the Lord. Later, I learned that her husband was an alcoholic. Instead of being bitter, she was a radiant Christian – a beautiful reflection of God's grace. She had learned to be content in the place where she was, depending on God to supply all her needs.

There was another lady whom I met at a Home Builders Wives' meeting in Memphis. I knew nothing about her family. One day my children and I were invited to a swimming pool where she and her teenage sons were swimming. I was astonished to see that both sons had muscular dystrophy! It was necessary for her to do everything for them – everything! And she did it with patience and grace. Obviously, she had accepted what God had given her; He knew she would be the perfect mother for these boys.

One of the best examples of being content regardless of the circumstances is writer and speaker Carol Kent. She wrote the book, *When I Lay My Isaac Down: Unshakeable Faith in Unthinkable Circumstances.* A few years ago I was privileged to meet and hear her, as she spoke at a Women's Conference in our Church in Sevierville, Tennessee. When I heard her story, I could hardly believe that this lovely and radiant Christian woman has a son who was convicted of first degree murder and is serving a life sentence without hope of parole because he killed the father of his step-children. Carol has refused to let this tragedy ruin her life. Instead, she focuses on God's goodness as she travels around the world telling women they can survive even the most horrendous of tragedies.

God's grace *is* sufficient! Refuse to allow unmet expectations to take you downhill on the D-road of Disappointment, Discouragement, Doubt, Disillusionment, Discontentment, Defeat, and Despair. My life verse is Jeremiah 32:17, which says, "Ah, Lord God! Behold, You have made the heavens and the earth by Your great power and outstretched arm. There is nothing too hard for You!" Nothing is too difficult for us to deal with, when we depend on God to carry us through!

Contentment is Not the Fulfillment of What You Want, But the Realization of How Much You Already Have (Author Unknown). [3]

CHAPTER 5

The Circle of Regret

Forgetting those things which are behind, and reaching forward to those things which are ahead, I press toward the goal for the prize of the upward call of God in Christ Jesus – Philippians 3:13b-14.

By this time, I am certain you have determined that I am a *senior* – one of those Senior Saints you see everywhere. I am not a member of the Blue Net Set, but for many years at my beauty shop, I did sit under a hair dryer for an hour each week. In those days, there was no such thing as a blow dry.

Why am I sharing all this information? Because my story took place on a day when I was sitting under one of those hair dryers at Blake's Beauty Shop in Memphis. Earlier that day, I had attempted to write an article for a Christian magazine but was distracted with worry about a situation involving my teenage daughter. Unable to concentrate, I found myself walking through the house thinking, "If only, if only, if only." I was truly in the Circle of Regret.[1]

Not accomplishing anything at home, I called the beauty shop to see if my beautician had an opening that afternoon. Thankfully, she was available. After my shampoo and set, I was seated under a big, black hairdryer. A friend came into the shop with a book in her hand. She walked up to my dryer, held up the book by a popular Christian author, and asked, "Have you read this book?" When I shook my head no, she offered it for my perusal.

As I turned the pages, nothing caught my attention until I saw the caption "God, Rescue Me From the *If Onlies*." I softly declared, "That's what I need. I need to be rescued from the *If Onlies*."[2]

On the way home from the beauty shop, the Holy Spirit convicted me that being in the Circle of Regret indicated my lack of faith in God! I was trying to handle this frustrating situation all by myself. How foolish our human reasoning can be.

When I got home, I hurried to the living room to kneel in prayer. I confessed to the Lord my sin of unbelief and received His forgiveness. In the next few moments, I became convinced of several things: I must <u>move from</u> <u>*If Only* to *Only God.*</u> Only God could have allowed this situation, and only God had the perfect solution to this problem. I was not to fret, but rather to "let Go and let God" handle the situation. God did work everything out for our daughter's good and His glory. Many times since that day, the Holy Spirit has prompted me to move from *If Only* to *Only God.*"[3]

> Move from *If Only* to *Only God.*

<u>When the Circle of Regret becomes</u> <u>my resting place, contentment flees</u> <u>out the door.</u> The nagging phrase, "if only," seeks to control my thought processes. On that particular day, I was worried about my daughter. Unfortunately, sometimes I am in the Circle of Regret because of unhappiness with myself. Dissatisfaction with the way I respond or perform, or with a bad decision I have made, can cause my regret to turn to despair.

> When the Circle of Regret becomes my resting place, contentment flees out the door.

In a devotional entitled, "Taking the Initiative Against Despair,"[4] Oswald Chambers gives the example of the disciples in the Garden of Gethsemane falling asleep instead of keeping watch for their Lord. He writes:

> "In the Garden of Gethsemane, the disciples went to sleep when they should have stayed awake; once they realized what they had done, it produced despair. The sense of having done something irreversible tends to make us despair. We say, 'Well, it's all over and ruined now; what's the point of trying anymore.' But Jesus comes to us and says, in essence, 'Sleep on now. That opportunity is lost forever, and you can't change that. But get up, and let's go on to the next thing.' If we are inspired by God, what is the next thing? It is to trust Him absolutely and pray on the basis of His redemption."

At the end of the devotional, Chambers admonishes us: "Never let the sense of past failure, defeat your next step." [5]

Just as we have to forgive others for not meeting our expectations, we have to forgive ourselves. When you feel you have failed to measure up, ask for God's forgiveness, seek to forgive yourself, close the door to the Circle of Regret, and move on to the next step. "Forgetting those things which are behind you," press on toward God's goal for you, trusting Him to lead you all the way.[6]

If You Want to Learn to Be Content, "Never Let the Sense of Past Failure, Defeat Your Next Step."[7]

Expectations

Frances A. McDaniel

A moment in time brought my world to a halt.
Accusations were made, who was really at fault?
Through it all, burdened down with grief and shame,
Knowing things might never be quite the same.
Have mercy, O Lord—I'm hard pressed and worn.
My dreams have been dashed, all shattered and torn.
Good intentions back lashed like a slap in the face.
Were those expectations so grossly misplaced?

Though weary and tired, help me, Lord to obey,
Seek Your infinite wisdom – walk on the way.
Complete your good work, transform and refine,
Intervene by Your grace, Sovereign Savior Divine.
You alone are the help of my countenance and soul,
Mighty Redeemer, Good Shepherd of old.
None other is worthy of trust, honor, and praise.
Glory to God is the banner I raise.

I will lift up my eyes unto God, I will look,
Set my affections on Him not this barren dry brook.
Expectations must be in my Lord and none other,
He alone is more faithful than sister or brother.

Surrender to Him by sheer will and design,

Trust His pulsating love to restore and refine.

His ways, though mysterious, are perfect and right,

The just live by faith and press on in the light.

My shield and reward are God Himself alone,

It shall come to fruition the good seed that was sown.

The Lord will perfect and turn all things around,

In His time and in stillness, salvation is found.

Sing to the One ever true and so faithful,

Rejoice, praise the Lamb with a heart that is grateful.

"For eye has not seen nor ear ever heard,"

The wondrous things He soon will cause to occur.[1]

Psalm 62: 5 NJKV

CHAPTER 6

Perplexing People

*...to the praise of the glory of His grace, by which He has
made me accepted in the Beloved* – Ephesians 1:6

No matter how young or old we may be, no matter where we
live or work, no matter where we go to church or who our
friends are, perplexing people will be present in our lives –
friends or acquaintances who hurt us, criticize us, or exclude
us. It is easy to lose our contentment when we are criticized or
excluded. Max Lucado says: "Every day God tests us through
people, pain or problems."[2] What are we to do? How are we
to respond?

As a young mother, I remember the day I was not invited to an event attended by many of my close friends. I did not learn that I had been excluded until later that afternoon when a friend called to ask why I had not been there. After hanging up the phone, I walked into my living room and sat down on the sofa. As I looked out the window, hurting inside and trying to determine why I had been excluded, God sent me to His Word – to Ephesians 1: 6 which says, "…to the praise of the glory of His grace, by which He has made me *accepted in the Beloved.*"

You and I are *accepted in the Beloved* – accepted by God because, as born-again believers, we are "in Christ." God loved us so much He sent His Son to die for

If you belong to Jesus, you can never be a reject!

us. <u>If you belong to Jesus, you can never be a reject!</u> God accepts you because of what Jesus did for you on the cross. If you have received Jesus Christ as your Savior and Lord, you are "in Christ," and Christ is in you in the Person of the Holy Spirit. Colossians 1: 27 says, "…Christ in you the hope of glory."

It's not *who* you are, but *whose* you are that truly matters. You are a person of worth, no matter who rejects or excludes you, or finds you unacceptable. You are God's child who is "hidden with Christ in God." Colossians 3:3 states: "For you died, and your life is hidden with Christ in God." What a blessing!

In spite of the truths of these wonderful verses in Colossians, there will be times when a relationship breaks apart because of an offense. When this happens, what are some steps we can follow in seeking to restore a broken relationship?

1. First, take the problem to Jesus. Talk to Him about the relationship. Think it through.
2. Go to God's Word and listen to His voice. If God reveals something to you, ask His forgiveness; then seek His guidance as you attempt to make things right. Go to the person, if possible, to ask his or her forgiveness. Reconciliation should be the goal.
3. Sometimes the other person will not acknowledge a problem. If this happens, it is important to seek to forgive that person, praying for him or her daily. Ask God to help you view this person from His perspective; pray that He will give you His love for them. It is true that you and I cannot control another person's actions or attitudes, but we can control *our* actions, *our* attitudes, and *our* responses.

> It is true that you and I cannot control another person's actions or attitudes, but we can control our actions, our attitudes, and our responses.

4. Remember that it is possible to be oversensitive to what others say or do. Sometimes we have what the Bible calls *vain imaginations* (Romans 1: 21). We imagine that things are wrong when they are not. As my husband has told me for years, "Assume the best." Then give your expectations to God.

Psalm 62:5, "My soul, wait silently for God alone, For my expectation is from Him."

Here is Susie's story (not her real name):

"Years ago, when I was very young, I was best friends with someone who moved away for a short time. When she came back to our town a few years later, something had changed. As I listened to her words and observed her actions, it was obvious she no longer wanted to be close friends. Immediately I asked myself, *'What have I done to cause this? What should I do about it?'*

I made a huge mistake – I talked with other friends of ours about the situation. That only made things worse. A few months later, I went to her home to talk with her. (That is what I should have done after I prayed earnestly about our broken relationship. It was a matter between the two of us that did not involve anyone else). When I inquired as to what I had done to hurt our relationship, she would not acknowledge that anything was wrong. We discussed the situation for a long time, but nothing was resolved.

Our relationship continued to deteriorate. In the days that followed, being in her presence left me depressed, upset, and angry. Why was I angry? Because she would not admit that a problem existed. One day, in desperation, I knelt by my prayer chair and cried out to the Lord as to what I should do. Instead of letting me rehearse the ways *she* had hurt me, God pointed His finger at *me*. He led me to Ephesians 4:31-32: "Let all bitterness, wrath, anger, clamor, and evil speaking be put away from you with all malice. And be kind to one another, tenderhearted, forgiving one another, even as God in Christ forgave you."

At that moment, I came face-to-face with the fact that I had allowed myself to become a bitter woman. The Holy Spirit so convicted me, I could hardly bear it. It took me a long time to confess my sins that morning. I knew I needed to get right with the Lord. Through His Word, God admonished me to be kind, tenderhearted, and forgiving. That day, I did forgive my friend. She might never acknowledge that our relationship was broken, but that did not matter. What mattered was my forgiveness of her. God had forgiven me for greater offenses; how could I not forgive her for this slight offense?

From that time forward, I did not talk to anyone but the Lord about our relationship. I said only good, positive things about her to other

> Return blessings for insults.

people. There was something else I felt led to do – return blessings for insults. 1 Peter 3: 8-9 admonishes us: "Finally, all of you be of one mind, having compassion for one another; love as brothers, be tenderhearted, be courteous; not returning evil for evil or reviling for reviling, but on the contrary, blessing, knowing that you were called to this, that you may inherit a blessing." I attempted to demonstrate love and compassion on a regular basis. Over time, our relationship started improving. Eventually, our close friendship was restored.

That was over forty years ago. There has never been a problem between us since that day. I am truly thankful God taught me those hard lessons when I was young and immature. Now that I am older, they are still relevant!"

"*Choose not to be offended; rather, seek to understand.*" - Fran McDaniel [3]

CHAPTER 7

The Pressure Cooker

We are hard-pressed on every side, yet not crushed; we are perplexed, but not in despair – 2 Corinthians 4: 8

Have you ever used a pressure cooker? Once, when I was a little girl, my mother placed a can of Carnation milk in her pressure cooker to caramelize it. That obviously was not its intended use. It wasn't long until the pressure was so great, the can exploded, lifted the lid off the cooker, and spread caramel all over the kitchen walls and ceiling!

Women usually have two reactions to pressure: When the pressure becomes unbearable, one personality type may explode. The other personality type will attempt to bury her many concerns. If she doesn't deal with her pressures, however, what's down in the well may come up in the bucket!

The apostle Paul is our Biblical example of one who was under great pressure. In 2 Corinthians 1: 8-9 he tells us, "For we would not, brethren, have you ignorant of our trouble which came to us in Asia, that we were pressed out of measure, above strength, insomuch that we despaired even of life. But we had the sentence of death in ourselves, that we should not trust in ourselves, but in God who raiseth the dead" (KJV).

Paul was *pressed out of measure*. He was completely overwhelmed; the pressure seemed more than he could bear. Have you ever been there – feeling like you would not *make it*? One of my favorite commentaries on this passage is by Dr. Sidlow Baxter in his outstanding devotional book, *Awake My Heart*.[1] He states:

> "Much of the pressure today is the product of uncertainty. Uncertainty engenders anxiety. Below the surface of many lives today there is a state of chronic suspense arising from a sustained chain of uncertainties. Life itself becomes anxious. Anxiety breeds worry. Worry means tension, strain, pressure. Paul's expression was: 'pressed out of measure.'

"Much of the pressure today is the product of uncertainty."

Pressed out of measure – take that word with its prefixes – depressed, suppressed, repressed, oppressed. All these are states into which the Adversary – the Devil, would bring us through pressure.

The Prince of Evil has made Christ's people his priority target these days, seeking to wear out our patience, disturb our peace, smother our joy, undermine our spirituality and silence our witness. His device is to preoccupy the mind with cares and swerve the gaze away from Christ."

In 2 Corinthians 4:7, Paul describes his pressures more fully, "We are pressured in every way, but not crushed; we are perplexed but not in despair; we are persecuted but not abandoned; we are struck down but not destroyed." Let's compare Paul's pressure-filled situation with some of our own circumstances.

First, Paul tells us that he was "pressured in many ways, but not crushed." All of us are under some pressure or stress. We women seek a variety of ways to make life less stressful. We walk, we run, we work out at the gym, we read a good book, we go shopping or on a trip, and we eat, eat, and eat! (I love the sign I saw in a restaurant the other day: "Stressed spelled backward spells Desserts").

But truthfully, we know that none of our attempts to relieve stress will be permanent; at some time, we will have to face reality. It is our choice to let the stresses overwhelm us, or through Christ, gain victory over them. Only God can make a way when it seems there is no way. He may not make a way *out* of these pressures, but you can be certain He will make a way *through* them, as you depend on His amazing grace. <u>When we choose to trust God, we can find contentment, even in our difficult, pressure-filled circumstances.</u>

> When we choose to trust God, we can find contentment, even in our difficult, pressure-filled circumstances.

Secondly, Paul was "perplexed, but not in despair." Perhaps you feel perplexed because you've tried so hard to be what God wants you to be, and you can't seem to please everyone. Women who are perfectionists have an especially difficult time when someone is critical of their performance or behavior. They often attempt to perform perfectly to gain the approval of others.

You may be perplexed because of an experience you are going through – it may make no sense at all. I remember a morning when I was perplexed about something, I wrote pages in my Prayer Journal, telling God I simply didn't understand why something was happening. In my devotional book at the bottom of the page was the Scripture reference, Isaiah 29: 16. The HCSB translates it this way:

> You have turned things around, as if the potter were the same as the clay. How can what is made say about His maker, 'He didn't make me?' How can what is formed say about the One who formed it, "He doesn't understand what He is doing"?

The message from God was loud and clear – I did *not* have to understand all that God allowed in my life. I needed to remember that everything that comes into the life of a child of God is "Father-filtered" (Author Unknown). I fell to my knees and asked God's forgiveness; He was indeed the One who made me – He was the Potter, and I was simply the clay!

Like Paul, refuse to despair – there is still hope. Use those pressures as an opportunity to trust God; leave room for His working. Remember: you will never be accepted by everyone, but you *are* accepted by God in His Beloved Son!

Third, Paul was "persecuted, but not abandoned." When you feel persecuted, perhaps you need to be reminded that God promises never to leave you or forsake you. He tells us in 1 Corinthians 10:13, "No temptation has overtaken you except such as is common to man; but God is faithful, who will not allow you to be tempted beyond what you are able, but with the temptation will also make the way of escape, that you may be able to bear it."

More than likely, none of us will be faced with the types of persecution Paul faced. We may, however, be "persecuted for righteousness sake."[2] When that happens, we need to commit the situation to God and seek His wisdom. When Jesus was reviled, 1 Peter 2:23 tells us: "He did not revile in return; when suffering, he did not threaten but committed Himself to the One who judges justly" (HCSB). Jesus set the example for us to follow – when persecuted, we are not to retaliate, but "commit ourselves to the One who judges justly."³

Fourth, Paul was "struck down, but not destroyed." We can easily feel devastated by someone's unkind words or actions. Often, it may be a member of the family who is causing grief. What is our first response when that happens? To strike back at the person who has hurt us? God's way is to "return blessings for insults, that you may inherit a blessing" (1 Peter 3:9). Return blessings for insults and pray, pray, pray. We must not let these hurts discourage us to the point of destroying us physically, mentally, or spiritually. (In serious circumstances where physical hurt is involved, it is important for the woman to seek qualified help immediately).

For a moment, let's go back to Paul's statement in 2 Corinthians 1: 9, "However, we personally had a death sentence within ourselves *so that we would not trust in ourselves, but in God who raises the dead.*"

Dr. Selwyn Hughes said in *Every Day Light*, "God knocks the props out from under us *so that we will rest our weight fully on God.*"⁴

Here are the words of two saints of God: Paul, a saint in the New Testament, and a modern-day saint named Selwyn Hughes. Both are proclaiming an essential truth: God allows trials so that we will learn to rely on Him--to trust *Him* to handle our problems. Adversity always has a purpose. If God can raise the dead, surely He can get me through this trial. I must yield the difficulty to Him and allow Him to release His power in my situation.

I have some dear friends in Tennessee who trusted God in the midst of frightening circumstances. They appropriated God's power as they stood between life and death. Here is their story:

"On January 16, 2015, I had just returned home from a grandson's basketball game and gotten ready for bed when a robber burst through our back door; instantly my husband was face-to-face with him and a gun in his face. The robber said, 'Give me your money and your jewelry or I will kill you.' He began to push my husband back into the bedroom where I was, while he was yelling obscenities at me. I remember thinking I must be having a nightmare. Our dog was barking, and he pointed his gun at her and threatened to kill her. He hit her, and thankfully, she was so frightened she went upstairs and never came down.

He kept the gun pointed at one of our heads the entire time and continually threatened to kill us. At one point he put the gun in my face and asked, 'Do you believe I will kill you?' I responded, 'If you did, I know where I am going. I will be in heaven with Jesus.' I told him repeatedly I was praying for him. My husband began to share with him, and he seemed to calm down. He told us he knew about Jesus, and he didn't want any part of it.

I never believed he was going to kill us. I could see angels all around protecting us. I was never afraid of him. My faith was so strong, and we felt the presence of the Holy Spirit all around us. After taking our jewelry and what cash we had, he forced us into our car. My husband drove, and I sat in the back seat with him and a gun in my ribs.

He told my husband, 'If you make one move that tries to alert someone to help you, I will kill your wife.' At that point, we didn't know if he would put us out and take the car or kill us. I continually prayed for him, and he knew it. After driving us about fifteen minutes from our home, he told my husband to stop the car and he looked at me and said, 'I am sorry I robbed such nice people.' He got out and ran. He has never been caught, and the things he stole have never been found.

I cannot explain how we knew what to do or how we stayed so calm other than it was God Himself that protected us. The police said, 'Because you were so calm it probably saved your lives.' I read Psalm 56 every day focusing on Verse 31, 'In God I have put my trust: I will not be afraid of what man can do unto me.' I have learned a lot, I have struggled a lot, I have been angry, and I have felt violated and scared of the dark. The thing I am most grateful for is to know my faith is real; and a robber or anything else can't take that away from me. We pray continually for his salvation and for him to be caught before he hurts someone. There is power in the name of Jesus and we used His name every chance we had with this man. To God be the glory." P.M.[5]

The extraordinary power that was released in our friends' situation did not come from their own resources. It came from God. Paul says in 2 Corinthians 4: 7, "Now we have this treasure in clay jars so that this extraordinary power may be from God and not from us." As Christians, we have the Holy Spirit living within us – He is our treasure – He lives within us to empower us to be overcomers.

Listen to Paul's prayer in Colossians 1: 9-11,

> "...we do not cease to pray for you, and to ask that you be filled with the knowledge of His will in all wisdom and spiritual understanding; that you may walk worthy of the Lord, fully pleasing Him, being fruitful in every good work and increasing in the knowledge of God; strengthened with all might, according to His glorious *power*, for all patience and longsuffering with joy"

That night in Germantown, Tennessee, the Holy Spirit "strengthened my friends with all His might, according to His glorious *power*, for all patience and longsuffering with joy." He enabled them to have victory in the midst of nightmarish circumstances. Why not ask the Holy Spirit to "strengthen you with all might, according to His glorious *power*, so that you will have patience and longsuffering with joy?"[6]

His grace is sufficient for my needs; His power is made perfect in my weakness! 2 Corinthians 12:9

Chapter 8

Disruptive Moments

And we know that all things work together for the good of those who love God: those who are called according to His purpose – Romans 8:28 (HCSB)

Women experience many disruptive moments in their lives, both major and minor. It may be something as minor as having a bad hair day or misplacing your glasses, or as major as having a car accident or learning that a family member has cancer. Each disruptive moment presents us with a choice: How will I respond? Will I despair or will I choose to trust God?

One Christmas, I experienced a major *disruptive moment*. I had a choice to make…trust the Lord or give into despair. Here is my story:

As is true for millions of other Christian women, a Christmas wreath on the front door has been an essential part of my Christmas decorations. It is a symbol of everlasting life through Jesus Christ, and the unending love of our Heavenly Father in sending His Son to die for each one of us. Every year I attempted to hang my Christmas wreath as soon after Thanksgiving as possible. On December 1, 2002, I was highly motivated to put a Christmas wreath on the front door of our house in Cordova, Tennessee.

In the late afternoon of November thirtieth, we returned to Cordova from a happy Thanksgiving Day celebration in Atlanta with our children and grandchildren. As we drove through our neighborhood, I noticed that almost all of our neighbors' front doors were adorned with Christmas wreaths. Our house appeared to be the only one with a Thanksgiving wreath on the door. I determined that the next afternoon, which was Sunday, I was going to remedy that situation. It was time to start decorating!

By Sunday afternoon, we were feeling the effects of a holiday weekend of travel, fellowship, and overeating. To say the least, we were tired! After church, Roland and his Mom set out for

Clarksdale, Mississippi, sixty miles south of Memphis. As they were exiting our house, Roland called to me and said, "You are tired; you don't *need* to go up in the attic and get those Christmas decorations!" Looking back, I'm sure I should have interpreted his words as a loving directive from my Spiritual leader. Unfortunately, I interpreted his statement as a loving suggestion – as something I didn't *need* to do. As the afternoon passed, my energy returned.

Suddenly I felt a *need* to replace the outdated Thanksgiving wreath on our front door with a Christmas wreath. I was not content to let things stay as they were. Quickly, I went upstairs to the attic where the Christmas decorations were stored.

At that juncture of our lives, we lived in a new house which had a partially floored attic. To give us more storage space, the contractor had built a platform approximately 8'x10' above the rafters. Five steps led to this raised area. When I entered the attic, I turned on the not-so-bright light. Walking to the edge of the platform, I climbed the steps. Immediately in view were the boxes and bins filled with Christmas decorations. Finding the wreath and some garland, I made two trips downstairs. After the second trip, I decided I'd done enough – this was not the day to complete my decorating!

Unfortunately, in my haste, I had left a mess in the attic; one of my new resolutions was to keep the attic in this house straighter than the last one. I hurried up the stairs to straighten the boxes and bins. (There was an important fact about the attic I did not know. The builder had made the back section of the platform, only half as wide as the front part). Although I thought I was in the middle of the platform, I was standing close to the edge. As I pushed a plastic bin into its slot, I stepped back to look for the lid, not realizing that my foot was resting on nothing but air. Instinctively, I pulled back my other foot.

That's when I realized I was falling. I reached up and grabbed the edge of the platform (now at eye level), but could not hold on. I heard myself saying, "I can't hold on!" As I continued my fall, having no idea where I would land, I lifted my hands above my head, closed my eyes, and cried aloud, "Lord, help me!" The next thing I knew I had crashed through the ceiling in our bedroom and landed on my right foot on the bedroom floor. It was soon apparent that I had injured my foot. Looking up at the ceiling, I saw the hole I had come through and cried out, "Lord, what have I done?!" I found out later I had fallen fifteen feet from the attic to the bedroom floor!

Just then the phone rang. Because my foot was hurting, I crawled across the bedroom floor to answer the phone. By the time I got there, the caller had hung up. I assumed it was Roland; he usually let the phone ring only four times. Not thinking clearly, I crawled into the kitchen to get my cell phone to call him back. When I reached him, he told me he was leaving Clarksdale, headed back to Memphis. It would take him an hour and a half to get home.

How am I to break my bad news to him? I wondered. I knew I had to tell him what had happened, but oh, how I dreaded that. Hesitantly, attempting to sound calm, I said, "Honey, I have to tell you something... I just fell from the attic through the ceiling into our bedroom and landed on my right foot! I think I hurt it in some way."

On the other end was silence. Roland could not believe what he had heard me say! At that moment, he experienced every emotion – fear that I had really messed myself up physically; helplessness that he was an hour and a half away and could not help his wife of forty plus years; anger that I had gone into the attic when he had told me I didn't need to; and anxiety as to what we should do. In the end, he told me to call our next door neighbor. Her husband was sick with a virus, so Yvonne came over by herself.

She began to help me think what to do next. (We should have called 911). We decided to call our new next door neighbors whom I had met only an hour before. Arlene and Tony came immediately, filled with compassion and concern. Tony kept asking, "Are you sure you aren't hurting anywhere besides your foot?" (He told me later he was worried about me because everyone he knew who had fallen from the attic had been hurt badly or killed).

Their son-in-law was visiting them; they called for him to come over. This strapping young basketball coach easily hoisted me up from the floor and took me to Arlene's car. She drove me to Baptist Hospital. The Emergency Room was extremely busy; the attendant placed me in a wheelchair with ice on my foot. Tony came to the hospital later. Roland actually made it there in about seventy-five minutes even though there was really no need to hurry. For four hours, I sat in the emergency room in that wheelchair! I was the third person in the emergency room who had fallen from the attic that day. The other two were also getting out their Christmas decorations.

As I sat there, I realized I had a choice to make. It was a choice I had heard described in a book by James Dobson entitled *When God Doesn't Make Sense*. There was a principle in the book that had grabbed my attention. Because I could not remember the exact quote, I had summed it up in my own words: <u>When a Christian is faced with a trial, he has two choices – to despair or to trust God. There is really only one option for the Christian…to trust God.</u>[1] I had just taught my daughter's Sunday School class that morning on "Trusting God." Now, I was faced with some decisions: Was I

> When a Christian is faced with a trial, he has two choices – to despair or to trust God. There is really only one option for the Christian…to trust God.

going to practice what I preached that morning? Was I going to despair? Or was I going to trust God? The choice was mine.

When I had made my decision, I prayed silently: *Lord, I am going to choose to trust You on this one. I am not going to despair. In fact, I am going to praise You in this crisis. I think that only my foot is hurt. I could have broken my neck or my back. I praise You that when I fell, I missed both the dresser and desk by a mere four inches. When I landed on the carpet, my tennis shoes protected me from being hurt worse. I don't understand how or why this happened. If I was not submissive to my husband, please forgive me. I didn't think I was disobeying him at the time. I give this awful situation to You, Lord. Just help us all get through it. We want You to get glory from this accident. In Jesus' Name. Amen.*

When the doctor finally saw me, he called for x-rays. The verdict… my right heel was broken, but he had found no other problems. My son later told me, "Mother, you had only one squashed angel!" The nurses put a cast on my foot, gave me some crutches, and sent me home. I was soon to dispose of the crutches after falling twice trying to use them; I transferred to a walker and a wheelchair.

The orthopedic surgeon I visited the next week took off the cast and put me in a boot. He told me that at my age (a terminology I was to hear many times in the future), he did not want to do surgery. The heel would heal on its own! For the next three weeks,

I was to lie with my foot above my heart, boot on, even when trying to sleep.

That was when it dawned on me how inconvenient my little *slip up* was going to be – a *pain* for me as well as my husband – especially for my husband. It was the first week of December. I had done very little Christmas shopping – unlike many women, I always wait until December to do most of my shopping. I had done no holiday cooking, and there were only two decorated spots in our house – the mantle and the front door. Praise the Lord! There was a wreath on our front door!

I had to turn this major disruptive moment over to my Heavenly Father, trusting that He would provide. And how He did – through friends and family! For three weeks, meals were brought every day. A group of close friends came and decorated my Christmas tree and the rest of the house. Our daughter did the Christmas shopping. Roland learned how to use the washing machine and how to cook eggs! I had to lie on the sofa in our Hearth Room with my foot suspended in the air, watching everyone else do *my* jobs!

I had made the choice not to despair. I had chosen to trust God, and He was there for me every moment of those days. One tremendous evidence of His care was my lack of pain. I had no pain in that broken heel. The doctor could not believe it. He told me a heel break tends to be painful. That was God's gift to me during this crazy time of my life.

Another of God's *gifts* to me was a greater understanding of the word "submission." I thought I had that submission thing down pat! I had to learn the hard way that when my husband says I don't *need* to do something, he is really saying, "I don't want you to do that!" Therefore, my going up to the attic was, in reality, being unsubmissive. May I encourage you today to learn from my mistake – if your husband says you don't *need* to do something – you don't *need* to!!

In the weeks ahead, I progressed from the wheelchair to a walker to a cane. My heartfelt desire was to learn from this experience all God intended for me to learn. I had written a message entitled, "Disruptive Moments," with a focus on responding from God's perspective instead of our own. Now, I had the opportunity to see the fulfillment of that desire. It was imperative that I learn to be content in those difficult circumstances.

When trials and tribulations come into our lives, we have two options: *to despair* or *to trust God.* The only option for the Christian should be to *trust God!* In the hospital emergency room that day, I *chose* to trust God. That made all the difference in the next six months of recuperation. I did learn to be content, right where I was! That "faith test" became my testimony in the years that followed. Chuck Swindoll once said, "God gives us opportunities brilliantly disguised as impossible situations."[2]

Isaiah 26:3-4a reads, "You will keep him in perfect peace, whose mind is stayed (focused) on You, because he trusts in You. Trust in the Lord forever."

No matter how perplexing the circumstances, no matter how difficult the situation, I can—and I must—trust God!!

His Purposed Plan

Frances A. McDaniel

In the stripping trials of life, God has in view a noble end,

To make of you a glory crown, a royal diadem.

In the valley of the shadow, look to God and praise His name;

In darkest night, seek truth and light, God's righteous rule and reign.

Come boldly to the throne of God through Christ, our mercy seat,

Find grace to help in time of need, wait at His blessed feet.

Trust beyond all doubt, and know that all which touches you

Has first passed through the hands of God, the faithful One and
true.

His ways are just and righteous though you do not understand.

Fear not for He is with you and upholds you in His hand.

Cling to the One who proved His love on Calvary's distant hill;

Look up and live, believe to see the wisdom of God's will.

Although the way seems rugged, trust the One who forged ahead,

Abide in Christ, embrace the cross, be done with fear and dread.

In weakness be made strong to rise as though on eagle's wings,

Be lifted to a higher plane, rejoice in praise and sing!

Look beyond the here and now beholding Christ the conquering
King,

No good thing will He withhold from those who trust His lead.

Therefore walk worthy of His love; grace will meet your every
need.

Neither death, nor life, nor anything can stay His purposed plan,
For God is good and will see you through to that blessed Beulah
Land.[3]

Isaiah 62: 1-7

CHAPTER 9

The Necessity of Prayer

The prayer of a righteous man [woman] is powerful
and effective – James 5: 16 (NIV)

Since I am a PK, a preacher's kid, I did not have a large inheritance. There were no beautiful rings or fancy antiques for me to inherit, and the gold watches that belonged to the men in our family were stolen one Valentine's night while my mother was at church. Do I feel slighted? No, because the heritage I have is an intangible one that can never be taken away from me. I was raised in a wonderful Christian home with two godly parents. My mother left me a priceless legacy – a legacy of a life of prayer. You see, it was my mother, Mabel Odle, who inspired me to cultivate a lifestyle of prayer – with her lips and with her life.

I feel certain that most of you who are reading this book believe in prayer. Many of you are prayer warriors. I have discovered, however, that when our lives are filled to the brim – and that is true for many of us – it is easy to have misplaced priorities; sometimes we need to be reminded of the importance of prayer. Without a regular prayer life, there will be no real contentment. <u>Contentment comes when we have a right relationship with the Lord – that relationship is developed through prayer.</u>

> Contentment comes when we have a right relationship with the Lord – that relationship is developed through prayer.

In the area of prayer, my mother set a wonderful example for me; I wanted to set a similar example for my daughter. It was a big part of the legacy I wanted to leave her. I thought my prayer life was in pretty good shape until I had a wake-up call at a Bible Conference at our church, when my children were very young. Reverend Peter Lord from Titusville, Florida, was the speaker for the conference. At the first morning session, I slipped in late and sat near the back of the room. Rev. Lord was already at the podium informing the audience that he wanted to take a survey of the congregation. Then he gave the instructions. He said, "I want all of you to *stand* who spent more time reading the newspaper this morning than you spent in prayer." Chills ran up and down my spine! I was mortified! I had spent more time reading the newspaper than in prayer that morning! I could not lie!

Totally humiliated, I stood along with many others. When I had sat down, I made a resolution: "I never want to be in that category again! Prayer is to have preeminence in my life! I *will* cultivate a lifestyle of prayer." (Today, the survey question would likely be: "How many of you spent more time on your computer, I- Pad or cell phone than you did in prayer this morning?")

Often, I have been asked why it is so important to have a lifestyle of prayer. My first answer is this: God has commanded us to pray--we pray to be obedient to our Lord. But those things that God commands are the very things that are *necessary* for us to have fruitful, joy-filled lives. Often God's commands are accompanied by a promise. Jeremiah 33:3 says, "Call to me and I will answer you, and show you great and mighty things which you do not know."

Why pray? It is an act of obedience, and it is a necessity! I cannot do without it; my family cannot do without my prayers for them. We are instructed in 1 Thessalonians 5:17 to "pray without ceasing; for this is the will of God in Christ Jesus concerning you." We are encouraged in 1 Chronicles 16:11 to "seek the Lord continually." Colossians 4: 2 says, "Continue earnestly in prayer, being vigilant in it with thanksgiving."

When we pray, we glorify God through our praise and thanksgiving. In Psalm 50:23, God tells us, "Whoso offers praise glorifies me." Psalm 113:3 says, "From the rising of the sun until the setting thereof, His name shall be praised."

Why pray? That I might come to *know* God, as I commune with Him, read His Word, and listen to Him speaking to me. Moses prayed in Exodus 33:13 that God would show him His way so that he would *know* God and find grace in God's sight. In *Disciple's Prayer Life,* T.W. Hunt stated, "A personal knowledge of God is the most important element in learning to pray." [1] The more I know my God, the more I love Him, and the more I love Him, the more I trust Him.

That principle proved true for me when I met my future husband, Roland Maddox. On our second date, he told me he loved me and asked me to marry him, but I really didn't *know* him at all. To get to know him, I had to spend time with him. We began to date regularly – the more I knew about him, the more I cared for him. It wasn't long until I fell in love with him. The more I loved him, the more I trusted him and enthusiastically agreed to marry him.

Just as we cannot get to know people well unless we spend time with them, there is no way to know our God other than to spend time with Him. He knows all about us. He knows us and loves us; He longs for us to come into His presence and communicate with Him.

I think of many other *reasons* to pray:

> To confess our sins and receive forgiveness. "If we confess our sins, He is faithful and just to forgive us our sins and to cleanse us from all unrighteousness." I John 1: 9

> To ask for wisdom. "If any of you lacks wisdom, let him ask of God, who gives to all liberally and without reproach, and it will be given him." James 1: 5

> To seek God's help and strength. "Ask and it shall be given you, seek and you shall find; knock and it shall be opened unto you." Matthew 7: 7

> To intercede for others. "So I sought for a man among them who would make a wall, and stand in the gap before Me on behalf of the land..." Ezekiel 22: 30a

> To find joy. "In Your presence is fullness of joy; At your right hand are pleasures forevermore." Psalm 16: 11

> "Let the hearts of those rejoice who seek the Lord! Seek the Lord and His strength; Seek His face evermore." Psalm 105: 3-4

> To receive God's blessings. "But those who seek the Lord shall not lack any good thing." Psalm 34: 10b

> To hear a word from God. "He who is of God hears God's words;" John 8: 47

Henry Blackaby stated in *Experiencing God:*

> "You cannot know the truth of your circumstances until you have heard from God."[2]

If we are to hear from Him, we must do as James 4:8 states: "Draw near to God and He will draw near to you." The Holy Spirit will open our hearts to the truth. John 16:13 says, "However, when He, the Spirit of truth, has come, He will guide you into all truth."

These are *reasons* we need to pray. There are some *requirements,* however, for our prayers to be powerful and effective. James 5: 16 says, "The effective, fervent prayer of a *righteous* man [woman] avails much." The NIV translates this verse, "The prayers of a *righteous* man [woman] are powerful and effective." What does it mean to be a *righteous woman*? She is a woman who has been made "right with God" through the blood of Jesus Christ. A righteous woman does not become righteous by her own goodness. As she repents of her sins and receives Jesus Christ as her Savior and Lord, God clothes her with *His* righteousness. Then, and only then, is she made "right with God."

When we receive Jesus Christ as Savior and Lord, He takes up permanent residence within us in the Person of the Holy Spirit. We receive a new nature, but still have to contend with the old nature. We cannot lose our salvation, but because of our old nature, we will continue to sin. We need to confess our sins *up to*

date. Daily, we need to be certain there is nothing hindering our
relationship with our Heavenly Father.

Isaiah 59: 2 succinctly explains this principle:

> "Behold, the Lord's hand is not shortened,
> That He cannot save;
>
> Nor His ear heavy that He cannot hear.
> But your iniquities have separated you from your God;
> And your sins have hidden His face from you,
> So that He will not hear."

The Psalmist gives us further insight as he tells us in Psalm 66:18, "If I regard iniquity in my heart, the Lord will not hear me." You see, the effectiveness of my prayer life does not depend on the location of my prayer closet, or the position of my body, but on the condition of my heart.

> The effectiveness of my prayer life does not depend on the location of my prayer closet, or the position of my body, but on the condition of my heart.

Every day we need to examine our hearts to see if there are sins to be confessed. Then we must ask God to search our hearts for any sin of which we are unaware. We are to confess those sins to the Lord, naming them one by one, and asking His forgiveness.[1]

1 John 1: 9 assures us, "If we confess our sins, He is faithful and just to forgive us our sins and to cleanse us from all unrighteousness."

Our prayers need to be from a pure heart with faith. As stated in 2 Timothy 2:2, we are to "call on God out of a pure heart." Hebrews 11:6 says, "Without faith, it is impossible to please God."

It is truly important to get alone with God on a daily basis, where just the two of us are speaking and listening. However, one of the greatest blessings for the Christian woman is to pray *with* and *for* others. Everyone has problems – they just have different *brand names*. The greatest thing you can do for your friends during their times of pain, hurt, and frustration is to lovingly support them by praying with them and for them. Someone once said, "Intercession is love at prayer" (Author unknown).

You and I need someone to intercede for us, too. In fact, everyone needs an Aaron and a Hur. In Exodus 17, Joshua was fighting a battle with Amalek. Moses told Joshua that the following day he would "stand on the top of the hill with the rod of God in his hand," interceding for him. Verses 10-12 tell us:

> "And Moses, Aaron, and Hur went up to the top of the hill. And so it was, when Moses held up his hand, Israel prevailed; and when he let down his hand, Amalek prevailed. But Moses' hands became heavy; so they took a stone and put it under him, and he sat on it. And Aaron and Hur supported his hands, one on one side and the other on the other side; and his hands were steady until the going down of the sun." [1]

Joshua defeated Amalek, and the battle was won!

Yes, we all need an Aaron and Hur in our lives. God is looking for intercessors – for women who will stand in the gap on behalf of their families, their friends, their churches, and their world. When we pray, battles are won!

In his classic book entitled *Prayer*, Dr. O. Hallesby reminds us: "To pray is nothing more involved than opening the door, giving Jesus access to our needs and permitting Him to exercise His own power in dealing with them…to give Jesus permission to employ His powers in the alleviation of our distress."[3]

Our prayers bring God into the situation! Isn't it amazing that this power source is available to us! We dare not fail to access it. An excellent verse to memorize is Psalm 55:17: "Evening, and morning, and at noon, will I pray, and cry aloud, and He will hear my voice."

God has invited us to come boldly to the throne of grace, to summon His power for our personal problems and those of others. We are not to come timidly. We are not to come faintheartedly. We are to come boldly and expectantly, seeking His mercy and His help in time of need – asking Him to release His power in our situations (Hebrews 4: 16).

The *results* of prayer can be amazing. When we pray for our children and grandchildren, their lives are impacted. It is our privilege (and duty) to pray for our husbands, our children, and our grandchildren every day. In my daily prayers for my family, I pray that God will bind Satan away from each one of them and will order their steps in His Word, allowing no sin to rule over them (from Psalm 119:133). I often pray Colossians 1: 9-13 for my family. Patti Webb and I co-authored a book entitled *A Mother's Garden of Prayer;* it includes prayers for our children *from the womb to the tomb.* All prayers are paraphrased Scriptures, specifically focused on the different aspects of a child's life.[4] (It is now an e-book as well as a hard cover book).

Many times we have opportunities to pray with others for those outside our families. We could tell story after story of the wonderful ways in which God has worked in answer to our corporate prayers. Paul wrote in 2 Corinthians 1:11, "And you can join in helping with prayer for us, so that thanks may be given by many on our behalf for the gift that came to us through the prayers of many." Let me share a story of the *gift* God gave me through the prayers of many:

> It was May of 2000. The Billy Graham Crusade had come to Nashville. As a member of the General Committee, I was working on the Women's Event to be held at the Grand Ole Opry on a Saturday morning before the Crusade began. Gigi Tchividjian was our speaker and Cece Winans, our guest soloist. We called it "A Morning with Gigi and Cece."

My first assignment was to assemble a group of women to pray before and during the event. I felt led by God to ask pairs of women to take segments of fifteen minutes to pray before and during the event. A few weeks before the event, the chairman asked me to take over the leadership. We were expecting approximately five thousand women. The Roy Acuff Theatre had been retained to accommodate the overflow. It was my desire that Gigi and Cece make an appearance in the overflow auditorium, so that all those in attendance could see them in person. Since I planned to interview each one, it was necessary to get the interview questions approved by their agents. We made all preparations possible to ensure that this event was a success.

On the Friday morning before the scheduled event on Saturday, I received a phone call. It was Janet, the Chairman of our Committee. She had some startling news: Gigi had called to say that she could not come the next day – she needed to stay by the bedside of her mother, Ruth Graham! If you have ever faced a situation like this, you know the consternation we immediately experienced. Janet asked me to meet with the other women on the committee at the Billy Graham Headquarters at 1:15 that afternoon. Meanwhile, we began to call local speakers to determine if anyone was available.

When we gathered at the headquarters, our first order of business was to pray earnestly for God's guidance – we had not found a substitute. After our prayer time, several suggestions were offered. Interviewing Gigi by phone was suggested by a person who knew this to be possible at the Opry house. After a time of discussion, we called Gigi to inquire if she would be available and agreeable to do a telephone interview. Gigi readily agreed. The Opry House concurred with our plan, too.

When Janet got off the phone, she looked at me and said, "Sarah, you're the one who has the approved interview questions; you need to sit on the stage and do the interview with Gigi." I can assure you that the idea of my being on the stage of The Grand Ole Opry had never once crossed my mind!! But, at this moment, it appeared there was no other alternative. I consented to interview Gigi, and Janet asked me to give a Gospel invitation at the end of the interview.

The next morning at eight-thirty, our first two prayer warriors arrived at the Opry House. We informed them of the situation, expressing how greatly we needed their prayers. Two more ladies arrived at eight forty-five, followed by two more, shortly before nine o'clock. My fears began to dissipate – a supernatural calm enveloped me.

As we prepared for the nine-fifteen beginning, I was told that the sound man was anxiously looking for me. When he found me, he seemed quite apprehensive. In a very worried voice he asked: "Did you know that we could *lose* contact with Gigi after we connect with her by phone?" When I told him I was not aware of that possibility, he continued, "What are you going to do?" Even though he was a nervous wreck, I felt no fear or trepidation. I was filled with God's peace – the "peace that passes all understanding" (Philippians 4:7). I knew this peace was the result of the prayers of others.

I asked the technician what he thought I should do. He told me I could tap dance! When I told him I couldn't tap dance – I was a Southern Baptist – he grunted, having no other suggestions for me. (There is not a big problem with Baptists and dancing these days. As the daughter of a Baptist preacher growing up in the fifties, however, dancing was not a sanctioned activity for me).

What happened next can only be explained as a "God Thing!" After Cece Winans had completed her mini-concert, Janet and

I walked onto the Opry stage. There were approximately five thousand women in those two venues. I experienced no stage fright, only complete peace, coupled with the confidence that God was in charge. Janet introduced me and left the stage.

Seated in the middle of the empty Grand Ole Opry stage, I gave a short introduction, sharing about time I had spent with Gigi. Then I called out, "Hello, Gigi." There was silence. I filled in for a minute or two and called to her again. There was still no answer. (Later, Janet told me that during that time, they were 'going crazy' backstage). My church friends in the audience began to pray for me. Unbelievably, I still felt absolutely calm and totally at peace. To get the audience laughing, I told them the tap dancing story. Everyone laughed and seemed to relax.

Suddenly, I heard a voice calling, "Hello, Sarah." It was Gigi! The ladies clapped heartily! We never lost connection again. The women seemed content with hearing Gigi by phone instead of in person. I will be forever grateful to those women who came every fifteen minutes that morning to pray, as well as for the many others who were praying for the event. I still marvel at what God did for me that day! When people pray, God's power is released into the situation – I personally experienced His amazing grace and power that day!

Do You Want to Be Content? Cultivate a Lifestyle of Prayer!

Covid-19 cheryl Wartz friend Friday Shirley
Lisa Wilson has virus - Metroplex - Patti- Marge Helen
melanie - grocerie + stores - Service workers
today anarchy - world -tylenol - get tested
symptoms I wk - now Taylor & Jason - Small hus - Shelda
Linda D
Barbara
Linda C -
Churches - Clarissa Brian

CHAPTER 10

Praise the Lord, Anyway!

I will praise the Lord at all times; His praise will
always be on my lips – Psalm 34: 1(HCSB)

In Max Lucado's excellent book, *You'll Get Through This*, he calls for "a splash of gratitude with that attitude."[1] In the last few decades, gratitude has not been a dominant characteristic of our nation. But what about you and me? Have our lives been characterized by gratitude?

I confess that many times I have opened my prayers with "Lord, help me." It is my privilege, as His child, to ask for God's help, daily and hourly, if necessary. But should I not continuously thank and praise my Heavenly Father for all He has done for me? Oh, how He must long for us to have an attitude of gratitude – not just when we are praying, but in every situation we are facing. God's Word tells us, "In everything give thanks for this is the will of Christ Jesus for you"[2] (1 Thessalonians 5: 18).

Psalm 100 is one of the most familiar praise chapters in the Bible. When I was growing up, as well as with my own children, we read this Psalm every Thanksgiving Day. A few years ago, I realized what the Scriptures were really saying to me: *"Enter* His gates with thanksgiving, and *into* His courts with praise." Thanksgiving was to be my *entrance* into the Throne Room of God. His courts were to be filled with my praises. God was telling me how to *begin* my morning Quiet Times.

As Fran McDaniel says, "Thanksgiving is not to be just a one-day event, but a lifestyle."[2]

When I was a young mother, struggling with one child who was sickly and the other who was strong-willed, I was given two tangible

> As Fran McDaniel says, "Thanksgiving is not to be just a one-day event, but a lifestyle."

items that changed my perspective about praising God. One was a paperback book by Frances Gardner entitled *Praise the Lord, Anyway.*[3] The other was a picture of a duck with a broken wing standing in a pool of tears, a tear falling from his eye. The caption underneath read, "Praise the Lord, Anyway!" I learned much later that the Bible calls this "offering the sacrifice of praise." Hebrews 13:15 says, "Therefore, through Him, let us continually offer up to God a sacrifice of praise, that is, the fruit of our lips that confess His name" (HCSB).

I determined to adopt the motto, "Praise the Lord Anyway," as my own. Of course, I wasn't always successful. It seemed that praising the Lord was not the first thing that came to my mind when something bad or troubling happened in our family. I was continually reminded of the verse in Psalms in which God says, "Whoso offers praise, glorifies Me"(Psalm 50: 23a). Often when I had not praised God in the midst of my difficult circumstances, this verse or motto would flash through my mind.

All of us will face times when praising the Lord, anyway is truly a sacrifice. If we practice praising the Lord, anyway in times of discontentment and struggle, I believe our burdens will be lifted and our hearts, encouraged. Jehovah inhabits our praises (Psalm 22:3). When we praise the Lord, Satan has to flee!

Sometimes our situations are so challenging that we feel imprisoned – chained, if you will. Things are so dark we see no way out. I have found that when the chains of fear or anxiety seem to bind me, praising the Lord is the first step toward freedom from those chains.

A missionary, who was very discouraged and despondent, was visiting the home of another missionary friend. As he walked into the house, he noticed a plaque that read: "<u>Try Thanksgiving</u>." Is that not what we need to do in the midst of our hard circumstances? Offering the sacrifice of praise will lift our spirits as we turn our eyes from our circumstances and focus on God and His goodness to us.

One of my favorite Bible stories is found in 2 Chronicles 20. A "vast multitude from beyond the Dead Sea and from Edom" had come to fight against Jehoshaphat. He proclaimed a fast for all Judah and gathered the people to seek the Lord as to what they should do. I love these words from the prayer he offered in front of a huge crowd of his people:

> "LORD God of our ancestors, are You not the God who is in heaven, and do You not rule over the kingdoms of the nations? Power and might are in Your hand, and no one can stand against You…We will cry out to You because of our distress, and You will hear and deliver." Later on, in his prayer he prays, "For we are powerless before this vast multitude that comes to fight against us. We do not know what to do, but we look to You."[4]

The Bible tells us that "the Spirit of the Lord came on Jahaziel." He told the people, "This is what the LORD says, 'Do not be afraid or discouraged because of this vast multitude, for the battle is not yours, but God's.'"[5]

By the next morning, Jehoshaphat had received God's marching orders. It was an amazing battle plan. Jehoshaphat "appointed some to sing for the LORD, and some to praise the splendor of His holiness." Then we read:

> "When they went out in front of the armed forces, they kept singing, 'Give thanks to the LORD, for His faithful love endures forever.' The moment they began their shouts and praises, the LORD set an ambush against the Ammonites, Moabites, and the inhabitants of Mount Seir who came to fight against Judah, and they were defeated." [6]

There are many principles in this amazing story we can apply to our own lives. The battles we face are not ours, but God's. He has a battle plan for each of us, but we must seek His face and His will to know His plan. We must obey what He tells us, regardless of how unbelievable His instructions may be. That is where our faith enters the picture. And perhaps the most neglected part of our battle plans – praise and thanksgiving!

༄

The verse in James that begins with the words *"Count it all joy..."* (James 1:2), was a verse often quoted in Bible studies I attended as a young woman. The Holy Spirit convicted me of my need to put this into practice. James 1:2-4 reads, "My brethren, count it all joy when you fall into various trials, knowing that the testing of your faith produces patience. But let patience have its perfect work, that you may be perfect and complete, lacking nothing."

I cross-stitched a "Count it all Joy" plaque for my bedroom, using yarn to match the colors of the walls and the fabric of the bedspread and curtains. When it was framed and ready to hang on the bedroom wall, I couldn't do it. God knew I was still in the learning phase. Since I was not at the place God wanted me to be, I put it in a drawer. It took times of testing to come to the point where I could really *count it all joy.*

God used a recession to get my attention. My husband was a homebuilder. He had told me earlier that home building and real estate were the first businesses to be affected by a downward turn in the economy. He was right. We went through a recession in the seventies, eighties, and nineties. I learned that the best way to save money was to stay out of the stores. Because we didn't have anything extra to spend, I found the call of the mall less appealing than before. But to "Count it all joy?" When those difficult times descended upon us, I hadn't quite learned to follow that command.

Evangelist Ron Dunn had made a statement something like this, "Because God wants you to trust Him, He will see to it that you have to." During that first recession, when we were visiting friends at Christmas, God saw to it that I had to! Our Christmas had been meager that year – we were really into saving money. On the other hand, the dad in the family we were visiting was in a high-paying profession – one not affected by the economy at that point. I'll always remember sitting in their living room when one of the couple's children marched in, carrying some expensive gifts her mother had received for Christmas.

I remember feeling my heart sink. I certainly didn't want to "consider it all joy" right then. Oh yes, I was reminded that I needed to "rejoice with those who rejoice," but at the moment I wanted someone to comfort me and "weep with those who weep" (Romans 12: 17). Even though I knew my husband could not afford expensive gifts at that time, it was difficult for resentment not to gain a foothold in my heart (he did give me similar gifts years later).

On the way home from our visit, the Holy Spirit convicted me. It was as if God were saying to me, *"You are being disobedient. I will supply your needs. It is not My will for you to have expensive clothes or fine jewelry at this time. Those things do not bring contentment. Look to me to fulfill the deep longings of your heart. Praise the Lord, anyway, and you will move forward in learning to 'count it all joy'."*

It was at that moment that I needed to praise the Lord and put a wreath on the door of my heart and my home – a wreath of *acceptance*. I needed to concentrate on what I *did* possess. I needed to reflect on this quotation: "Contentment is not the

81

fulfillment of what you want, but the realization of how much you already have" (Author Unknown). I lived in a lovely home with a wonderful husband. It was not his fault the economy had tanked. We had never gone without a meal and were well off by the world's standards. Most of all, we belonged to Jesus, who would take care of us in good days and bad. I needed to learn to be content in my circumstances. My attitude of ingratitude must change to praise and thanksgiving. Praise the Lord, anyway!

When we got home, I opened the bed stand drawer to retrieve my wall plaque. Hastily, I hung it on the wall as a reminder to "Count it all Joy" no matter what! Today there is a painted plate on a shelf beside my breakfast table which gives me that same reminder each time I sit down to eat.

As Christian women, we must "walk by faith and not by sight" (2 Corinthians 5: 7). Our welfare is not dependent on the economy or the government. We are totally dependent on our Heavenly Father to make a way through any wilderness we have to pass through. We must be willing to accept His plans for solving our problems. No matter how dark it may be, somewhere the sun is shining. And always the Son is shining in our hearts. Put a wreath on your door – wherever you live and "count your blessings, naming them one by one."[7] Then praise the Lord, anyway and trust in the all-surpassing power of God to see you through.

I wrote this several years ago:

WHEN TRIALS COME,

Am I going to fall apart, or fall on my knees?

It is *my* choice!

Am I going to be filled with fear, or full of faith?

It is *my* choice!

Am I going to live in the Circle of Regret or give thanks in everything?

It is *my* choice!

Am I going to panic or will I "commit every detail of my need to God in earnest and thankful prayer," allowing "the peace of God to keep constant guard over my heart and mind through Christ Jesus?" Philippians 4:6-7 (NLB)

It is *my* choice!

In every situation, you and I have a choice in the way we respond. We can praise the Lord, anyway or we can grumble and complain. We can have a bad attitude or "a splash of gratitude."[8] It is our choice!!

Try Praising the Lord, Anyway!

CHAPTER 11

Do You Need a Rest?

Jesus said, 'Come unto Me, all of you who are weary and burdened, and I will give you rest' – Matthew 11:28

It is rare to find someone who doesn't need a vacation – a place to rest – at least periodically. The cares of this world are enormous and the pressures are so great, we can all benefit by getting away from the rat race. A health magazine arrived this week with an article that encouraged the reader to take time for a vacation. The article promoted the physical and mental benefits of getting away each year to rest.

Nearly every year our family vacations were at the beach or in the mountains. Both destinations were restful and enjoyable. Roland and I vacationed in the Smoky Mountains nearly every fall for over forty years. We loved the changing of the leaves, the mountain streams and beautiful vistas.

In 2003, we were fortunate to find an affordable condo overlooking Mount Le Conte, the highest mountain surrounding Gatlinburg, Tennessee. It was not a new place, but very well-built, and it had a million dollar view. Our family loved this mountain-top place of rest.

The first thing I did after moving in was to put a wreath on the door. It was a wreath with green leaves, decorated with assorted fruits. It would be suitable to use year round. We planned to visit our second home as often as possible. We located a wonderful church near Gatlinburg, the First Baptist Church of Sevierville. In that church, we found love, sound teaching and preaching, and excitement we had not seen or felt in a long time. Little did we dream the close connection we would soon have with this Church.

While rest is beneficial for our bodies, it is even more important for our souls. Jesus affirms that fact as He calls the people in His day, and us, to come to Him for rest. Of course, the *rest* He is speaking of differs from simply taking a vacation. It is a *rest* that can take place wherever you are, at home or away. In Matthew 11:28-30, listen to what Jesus says:

> "Come to Me, all of you who are weary and burdened, and I will give you *rest*. Take My yoke upon you and learn from Me because I am gentle and lowly in heart, and you will find *rest* for your souls. For My yoke is easy and My burden is light."

Vine's Expository Dictionary gives a definition of the *rest* Jesus is referring to in this Matthew passage. This word "rest" is from the Greek word *alapano*, which means "to repose, to refresh, to take ease, and to give or take rest." *Vine's Dictionary* comments: "Christ's *rest* is not a rest from work, but *in work*, 'not the rest of inactivity but of the harmonious working of all the faculties and affections – of will, heart, imagination, conscience – because each has found in God the ideal sphere for its satisfaction and development.'"[1] It is a faith rest, in which Jesus lifts our heavy burdens and fills us with His peace.

It was interesting to find the *Random House Dictionary's* definitions of *rest*. One definition was "mental or spiritual calm." Another definition was "relief or freedom, especially from anything that wearies, troubles or disturbs you."[2] We know that only Jesus can give us lasting mental and spiritual calm. Only Jesus can give us real relief and true freedom from those things that weary, trouble or disturb us. Isn't that what He promises us?

Looking at Matthew 11: 29-30 again, Jesus admonishes us, "Take my yoke upon you and learn from Me, and you will find rest for your souls. My yoke is easy and my burden is light." I love the yoke analogy Jesus used. In those days, oxen were the beasts of burden. Those listeners could easily identify with His analogy. The yokes the oxen wore were made of wood. The farmer would bring the ox to the carpenter to be carefully measured for the yoke. When the yoke was ready, the ox was brought back for a fitting. Needed adjustments were made to ensure that the yoke fit well.

When Jesus tells us, "take My yoke upon you," He is assuring us that the life He gives us will not be a burden to irritate us – the tasks He has for us are tailor made to fit us. William Barkley once said, "Whatever God sends us is made to fit our needs and abilities exactly. His burden is easy to carry – it is laid on us in love and meant to be carried in love."[3]

How do we take His yoke upon us? By submitting to His will for us. Just as the farmer controls the oxen by means of yokes, when we accept the yoke Jesus has designed for us, we are giving Him the controls of our lives – allowing Him to "work in us both to will and to do His good pleasure" (Philippians 2:13). By doing so, we will find the rest He offers us.

Major Ian Thomas came to our church many years ago to speak at a seminar. Several of his statements have stayed with me through the years. He suggested that when we face trials and temptations, we should declare, "Oh, Lord, I cannot. You never said I could. You can. You always said You would. I vacate and You occupy."[4] Then he asked us to claim the verse in Philippians 4:13 which states: "I am able to do all things through Him who strengthens me" (HCSB).

In the year 2000, a book containing Ian Thomas's works was published, entitled *The Indwelling Life of Christ – All of Him in All of Me*. This book contains an illustration that amplifies the teaching I recalled. He says:

> "Suppose you were digging a hole, and I offered to give you a rest... Obviously, there is only one way: You must get out and let me get in. You must drop the spade and let me pick it up. You must quit and let me take over. You must vacate that hole in the ground so I can occupy it. That is the way the Lord Jesus wants to give you and me rest."

When Jesus says, "Come unto me all you who labor...and I will give you rest," Dr. Thomas explains, "He is speaking to us just as He did to the hole digger. He is saying to us: 'Get out and let me get in. Vacate and let me occupy. Drop the spade and let Me dig!'"[5] Later on in the book he emphasizes that "Christian rest is not inactivity. Christian rest is rest because Jesus carries the load...it is the rest of faith."[6]

You and I can rest wherever we are if we will "let go and let God" handle our burdens. If we vacate our position of control and let Him occupy (have control), we will find rest for our souls. That rest will ensure contentment.

If I go to Jesus when I am weary and burdened, He will give me rest and enable me to learn contentment.

CHAPTER 12

The Reckoning

Likewise, you also, reckon yourselves to be dead indeed to sin, but alive to God in Christ Jesus, our Lord – Romans 6: 11

As I reflect on my journey from house to house and city to city, I have come to a conclusion about contentment. I believe you and I will be content *only* when the Holy Spirit is in control of our lives – when we are, as Galatians says, "walking by the Spirit" (Galatians 6:18).

What does it mean to "*walk by (or in) the Spirit?*" You and I received a new nature at the time of our salvation – a

> I believe you and I will be content only when the Holy Spirit is in control of our lives

divine nature. We are new creatures in Christ Jesus. But as long as we are here on this earth in these human bodies, we have to put up with our old self, our SIN nature – what the Bible often calls our *flesh*. That old man – that old nature – that thing we call flesh, wages war every day with our new nature. If the Holy Spirit controls our lives, then we walk in the Spirit; if the flesh controls the body, we walk in the lusts of the flesh.

We all have "I" problems. Not eye problems, but an "I" problem: *I, me, mine.* The Bible clearly states: "For all have sinned and come short of the glory of God" (Romans 3: 23). What is the middle letter of the word sin? A big "I."

How are we going to allow the Holy Spirit to have the control of our lives? The old nature, the flesh, the self, must be reckoned (counted as) dead. We must spend time with the Lord, examining our lives to see where the "flesh" is still in control. Sins of the flesh like pride, selfishness, self-pity, lack of gratitude, resentment and bitterness, can trip us up, causing us to be dissatisfied with the people around us, as well as with our circumstances. These sins of the flesh must be put to death. As Dr. Cal Guy once said, "We need to have our own funerals."[1]

I heard the story of an Indian, who was visiting with a friend. The Indian was attempting to explain to his friend what it was like to be a Christian. He told him, "It is like having two dogs who are always fighting – a black one and a white one – living inside you."

The friend asked him, "Which one wins?"

The Indian answered, "The one I feed the most."

What an excellent example of the war being waged between the old nature and the new.

Dr. Warren Wiersbe says, "Sin wants to be our master. It finds a foothold in the old nature, and through the old nature seeks to control the members of the body. But in Jesus Christ, the old nature was crucified." In other words, the power of sin was broken at the cross. He goes on to comment, "Sin and death have no dominion over Christ. We are 'in Christ,' therefore sin and death have no dominion over us."[2]

We know these are the facts, but how do we make this work in our daily experience? I believe there is a four-step process:

1. *Recognize* our sins. Romans 6: 12 admonishes us: "Do not let sin reign in your mortal body, so that you obey its desires..." If we desire to walk in the Spirit, the first step is to *recognize* the evidences of the flesh (self) that are in our lives – pride, discontent, self- centeredness, selfishness, lack of love, lusts of the flesh, etc. You may have to do as

I often do – get on your face before the Lord and ask Him to reveal to you the sins of which you are not aware. The Psalmist's prayer in Psalm 139: 23-24 is one I regularly pray, "Search me, O God, and know my heart; try me, and know my anxieties; And see if there is any wicked way in me…"

2. The second step is to *reject* these sins – agree with God that these sins of the flesh are in control and must be expelled from your life. Confess them one by one. "If we confess our sins, He is faithful and just to forgive us our sins, and to cleanse us from all unrighteousness" (I John 1:9).

3. Then *reckon* these sins to be dead – count them as dead to you. (To *reckon* is to act, or count on the fact that I am dead to sin and alive to Christ.)

Romans 6: 11-14 in the NKJV vividly describes this process and the next:

> "Likewise you also, reckon yourselves to be dead indeed to sin, but alive to God in Christ Jesus our Lord. Therefore do not let sin reign in your mortal body, that you should obey it in its lusts. And do not present your members as instruments of unrighteousness to sin, but present yourselves to God as being alive from the dead, and your members as instruments of righteousness to God. For sin shall not have dominion over you, for you are not under law but under grace."

J. B. Phillips paraphrases Romans 6:11 in this way, "In the same way look upon yourselves as dead to the appeal and power of sin but alive and sensitive to the call of God through Jesus Christ our Lord."[3]

Major Ian Thomas describes the process very clearly, "Consent, therefore, to die to all that you are which does not derive from all that Christ is, and thank Him for His willingness to make it real in your experience."[4]

4. ***Relinquish*** the control of your life and ***surrender*** to the control of the Holy Spirit. Romans 12:1-2 is a familiar passage to most Christians. It says:

"I beseech you therefore brethren, by the mercies of God, that you present your bodies a living sacrifice, holy, acceptable to God, which is your reasonable service. And do not be conformed to this world, but be transformed by the renewing of your mind, that you may prove what is that good and acceptable and perfect will of God."

To conclude this process, your prayer could be similar to this one:

I surrender to You, Lord Jesus, all that I am and all that I have. I accept Your plan for me. Holy Spirit, take control of my life. I want to walk in the Spirit, so I will not fulfill the desires of the flesh. I want to learn to be content in the state in which I am at this moment. I know I can because of this promise in Philippians 4:13: "I can do all things through Christ who strengthens me." In Jesus' Name, Amen.

Surrender fully to the control of the Holy Spirit

CHAPTER 13

A Divine Intervention

'...not My will, but Yours be done' – Luke 22:42 **

We had lived in Nolensville, Tennessee, less than two years when God called us to move again. My goodness! At my age, I never dreamed my life would be like this! I thought I would be settled somewhere for the rest of my life, enjoying Roland's retirement and our grandchildren. BUT GOD!! And oh, how God had been working in our lives! But I am getting ahead of myself.

For us, December 2008 and January 2009 are months that will forever hold a prominent place in our Museum of Memories. In the fall of 2008, the stock market crashed, and everyone was surveying his or her economic situation. We believed that we needed to downsize in our living space; however, we had no idea where that space should be!

We did not plan to return to Memphis. Nashville was a wonderful place to live, but it was not high on the list either. Regardless of its many positive qualities, it was never promoted as a place to retire. There was no compelling reason to remain there. What were we to do? Where were we to go? Having no answers, we did the only thing that was logical – we got on our knees and surrendered to the Lord, "Whatever, whenever, and wherever, You want us to go and do." It was the desire of our hearts to *finish well*. Roland had already retired twice. He wanted to keep working, but only God knew what was best. We had surrendered to the Lord for His leading and direction in our lives. We knew He would show us the way. God had promised in Psalm 32:8, "I will instruct you and teach you in the way you should go."

What happened next can only be described as a "God Thing!" I was preparing to facilitate a study of *Experiencing God* for a group of women in our neighborhood. To prepare for our January launch, I began studying the material in late December. Here are some statements from *Experiencing God* that caught my attention:

**Words spoken by Jesus in the Garden of Gethsemane, just before His death on the cross.

"When God is about to do something through you, He has to get you from where you are to where He is, so He tells you what He is doing. You cannot stay where you are and go with God."[1]

Two quotes by D. L. Moody: "One ordinary person in the hand of Almighty God can do *anything* God commands." "God wants you to be you and to let Him do through you whatever He chooses."[2]

"God never asks people to dream up something to do for Him... The pattern in Scripture is that we submit ourselves to God. Then we wait until God shows us what He is about to do."[3]

On the morning of January 14, 2009, this is what I read in *Experiencing God:*

"God has a right to interrupt your life anytime He wants to! He is Lord. When you accepted Him as Lord, you gave Him the right to help Himself to your life."[4]

On that day, my husband was having lunch with Rev. Randy Davis, pastor of First Baptist Church, Sevierville, Tennessee. They had become good friends while working on a denominational committee. During lunch, Randy presented an unbelievable proposal to Roland. God had laid Roland on his heart as a prospective Executive Associate Pastor for First Baptist. Randy asked Roland if he would be willing to submit his resume to the search committee responsible for filling this position. He would place it in the stack of resumes anonymously. In doing so, the committee would not be biased, and God would have full sway in the decision.

Roland was stunned! He was an ordained deacon, but not an ordained minister. Besides, he was seventy-two years old. How many churches consider a man his age for their ministerial staffs? As improbable as it seemed, when Roland informed me of Randy's request, we both knew this was God's doing. Roland was to submit his resume. We had surrendered to whatever, whenever, wherever. We would go to Sevierville if God were calling us there.

We soon realized the decision would not be made immediately. We must wait for God's answer. Over the next two months, the Search Committee received more than two hundred and fifty resumes for this position. By March, they had whittled the number down to thirty. My husband was still on their list. By May, there were only three left on the list. Roland was one of the three. For the first time, the committee asked Randy for his preference. The committee wisely interviewed all of the top three prospects.

We were asked to come to Sevierville for an interview on a Tuesday in May 2009. The committee was to vote the following Sunday. Pastor Randy asked them to vote by secret ballot. We were pleased with his decision, because we had agreed we should not go unless the vote of the committee was unanimous. On the

Sunday afternoon of the vote, while I was playing my piano in Nolensville, the Holy Spirit impressed me that the vote had been taken and was unanimous. A few hours later, we received a call telling us that the vote was indeed unanimous; they wanted us to come. Only God could have done this for us! We praised His Holy name again and again!

With a unanimous vote from both the deacons and the congregation, Roland began to serve on the staff of First Baptist Church, Sevierville, Tennessee, on June 30, 2009. We truly loved our three years there. It was an absolute gift from God! I experienced a level of contentment I had not known in years. What a joy it was to be able to serve Jesus in that church!

In this new position, Roland was able to use his experiences of the past fifty years. Our home church in Nashville ordained him to the Gospel Ministry in August of 2009. We lived in our condo in Gatlinburg instead of buying another house. We didn't have to put a wreath on that door – there was already one there.

This prayer from *31 Days of Praise*, by Ruth Myers, has become very special to me:

Thank You [Lord], that I can safely commit my location and situation to You...I rest in the fact that You have me in this place for this day... I praise You that You will faithfully guide me throughout life to just where You want me to be, as I seek to do Your will."[5]

Learning to Be Content Requires the Full Surrender of Our Lives to God

CHAPTER 14

The Satisfied Woman

A good man [woman] will be satisfied from above – Proverbs 14:14

Contentment

"We can learn contentment whether we are single or married, with career or without career. <u>Contentment from God's perspective cuts out the 'superwoman syndrome' and brings in the 'satisfied woman syndrome'.</u>" L. Jane Moline, *A Woman of Excellence.*[1]

The dictionary defines the word *content* as "satisfied" and "being at ease."[2] A satisfied woman is a woman who is at ease – she is not filled with anxiety or worry or

> Contentment from God's perspective cuts out the 'superwoman syndrome' and brings in the 'satisfied woman syndrome'.

fear. She has made a definite choice – a choice to accept her circumstances as coming from God, believing that God has her in that place for a purpose. When that purpose is fulfilled, He will remove her or lead her to a new abode. One of my favorite Psalms is Psalm 57:2 (HCSB): "I call to God, Most High, to God who fulfills His purpose for me..." He will fulfill His purpose for us if we are fully committed to Him.

During my personal journey, I've often asked myself, *"Am I a satisfied woman? Am I contented and at peace within?"* A contented woman is not dependent on anyone else for her satisfaction. She has not made her house, her financial situation, her husband, her children or her friends, slaves of her expectations. She is not a self-willed woman who wants her way all the time. She doesn't need abundant material things to make her happy. She has learned that contentment – being truly satisfied – comes from God and God alone. "My soul, wait silently for God alone, For my expectation is from Him..." (Psalm 62: 5). Contentment comes when a woman is fully yielded to the control of the Holy Spirit – when she has died to the flesh and surrendered to the Spirit.

> Contentment – being truly satisfied – comes from God and God alone.

Being a satisfied woman will not just affect you. It will make a difference in the lives of all those with whom you come in contact.

If you are a satisfied, contented woman, it will be revealed in your spirit. I Peter 3:4 speaks of "the unfading beauty of a gentle and quiet spirit, which is of great worth in God's sight" (NIV).

I love how the *Women's Study Bible* describes this verse:

"The hidden beauty of the heart is displayed by a gentle (meek) and quiet spirit. This quality is not a reference to genetically acquired personality traits, such as being a person of few words, but rather to an inner attitude marked by the absence of anxiety, coupled with a trust in God as the *Blessed Controller* of all things...A woman characterized by a gentle and quiet spirit is not only precious to God and a glory to her husband but also a joy to all who are around her."[3]

> A woman characterized by a gentle and quiet spirit is not only precious to God and a glory to her husband but also a joy to all who are around her."

Once I heard a speaker ask a group of young women, "Are people glad when you enter a room or relieved when you leave it?" Oh, me! How convicting! I know it is our desire to be "precious to the Lord, a glory to our husbands, and a joy to all who are around us,"[4] but that is not an easy task. Spending time in the presence of the Lord every day is absolutely essential for the Christian woman who desires to please her Lord!

I believe that God will enable you to be content wherever you are: in an apartment, a condo, a mansion, a jail, a women's shelter or wherever you may be at this moment. God is right there with you, ready to give you all the strength, patience, faith, endurance, grace, and peace that you need. Hebrews 4:16 says, "Let us therefore come boldly to the Throne of Grace, that we may obtain mercy, and find grace to help in time of need." It will come just at the time you need it. Why? Because wherever you are, He is there! He is Immanuel – God with us – at all times and in all places!

Years ago we had a fantastic women's conference at Two Rivers Baptist Church in Nashville, Tennessee. Our featured speaker was Ann Graham Lotz. At the beginning of the conference, long before Ann spoke, something happened that none of us will ever forget. Travis Cottrell, our Interim Music Minister at Two Rivers, had scheduled the church choir to sing for the opening session. When our pastor's wife completed the invocation, the audience was amazed to see the members of the church choir standing in each aisle throughout the auditorium. They interrupted that moment of silence as they began to sing:

HE IS HERE
He is here, Hallelujah! He is here, Amen!

He is here, holy, holy;

I will bless His name again. He is here, listen closely;

Hear Him calling out your name. He is here; you

can touch Him. You will never be the same.

L. Kirk Talley[5]

As they completed this beautiful song and began to move toward the choir loft, the presence of the Holy Spirit fell on that sanctuary in a miraculous way. At that moment we knew He was present with us – He was there!

Today, as you are reading this book, if you have received Jesus Christ as your Savior and Lord, you know that God is there with you, to sustain and encourage and guide. He is there for whatever you need. You can call out to Him – He knows your name and your need. He is there – praise Him aloud and bless His holy name!

(Please Note): If you have never had a personal encounter with Jesus Christ, may I encourage you *not* to spend another day without receiving Him as your Savior and Lord (see explanation below).

The contented, satisfied woman has an "inner attitude marked by the absence of anxiety, with a trust in God as the Blessed Controller of all things."[6] *If you have received Jesus Christ as Savior and Lord, you can learn to be content. The Holy Spirit will enable you to be!*

THE PLAN OF SALVATION

1. **God loves you and has an awesome plan for your life.**

   "For God so loved the world, that He gave His only begotten Son, that whoever believes in Him should not perish, but have eternal life" (John 3: 16).

   "For I know the plans I have for you—this is the Lord's declaration— 'plans for your welfare, not for disaster, to give you a future and a hope'" (Jeremiah 29:11 HCSB).

2. **Because all of us are sinners, alienated from God, we cannot experience God's love or know His plans for us until we receive Jesus Christ as Savior and Lord.**

   "For all have sinned and fall short of the glory of God" (Romans 3: 23).

   "For the wages of sin is death" (Romans 6: 23). This means we are spiritually separated from God. "There is a great gulf separating us from God; the only way to bridge this gulf is through Jesus' death on the cross for our sins."[7]

3. **Jesus Christ is God's provision for our sins.** He died on the cross to take upon Himself the punishment we deserved.

   "But God demonstrates His love toward us, in that while we were yet sinners, Christ died for us" (Romans 5: 8).

   No man or woman can come to God except through Jesus. He is the only way to God – no good works or any other means will provide a way to God. How do we know this to be true? Jesus said in John 14: 6, *"I am the way, and the truth, and the life; no one comes to the Father, but through Me."*

"For by grace you are saved through faith, and this is not from yourselves; it is God's gift – not from works so that no one can boast" (Ephesians 2: 8-9 HCSB).

4. Just knowing these facts is not sufficient. **We must personally acknowledge that we are sinners in need of God's forgiveness. We must repent of our sins.** To *repent* of our sins means to turn *from* them and turn *to* Jesus.

"If you confess with your mouth the Lord Jesus and believe in your heart that God raised Him from the dead, you will be saved" (Romans 10:9).

5. **Humbly come to Jesus Christ and admit that you are a sinner. Turn from your sins and seek His forgiveness. Turn your life over to Him, receiving Him as your Savior and Lord.**

The moment you receive Jesus Christ as your Savior and Lord you are *born-again* and receive eternal life. God's Word promises eternal life to all who receive Jesus into their hearts.

"For God so loved the world, that He gave His only begotten Son, that whoever believes in Him should not perish, but have eternal life" (John 3: 16).

"But as many as received Him, to them He gave them the right to become children of God, to those who believe in His name" (John 1: 12).

6. **At the moment of salvation, the Holy Spirit takes up permanent residence in your life.** He will "teach you all things" (John 14:26).

7. *Find a Christian friend with whom you can share your good news and pray.*

Questions for Discussion

Chapter 1 – A Life-Changing Experience

1. Is there an area of your life in which you are experiencing discontentment? (Personal)
2. How do we learn to be content?
3. Is there anywhere you need to put a literal or figurative wreath on a door to symbolize *acceptance*? On the door of your home? On the door of your church? On the door of your child's room? On your bedroom door? (Personal)

Chapter 2 – An Eye-Opening Walk

1. Why is the symbolism of wreaths important? Which symbol means the most to you?
2. Do you have a wreath or other decoration on your front door?
3. Is there something in your life you are having a difficult time accepting?
4. Ask the Lord to help you accept those things He has provided for you. (Personal)

Chapter 3 – God's Waiting Room

1. Are you in God's Waiting Room today? Are you content?

2. What, for you, is the most difficult part of being there?

3. If you have previously been in God's Waiting Room, please share how God brought you through this time in your life.

Chapter 4 – Unmet Expectations

1. What are some of your unmet expectations? How are you handling them?

2. What does God's Word tell us about our needs? Do you really believe He will meet all your needs? Can you give a testimony from your life or someone else's?

3. How would you define *grace*? What does God tell us in 2 Corinthians 9:8? What does that mean to you?

4. Will you choose one of your unmet expectations, reduce it to zero and give it to God?

Chapter 5 – The Circle of Regret

1. When you don't live up to your own expectations, what is your usual response?

2. Tell about a time you were *resting* in the circle of regret.

3. What do you think of Oswald Chambers' advice?

4. Are the words "if only," a frequent part of your thinking or conversation? What does this indicate about your faith in God's sovereignty?

5. Will you make a determination today to "forget those things which are behind and do the next thing"?

Chapter 6 – Perplexing People

1. What did you take away from this chapter? Did you learn something helpful about relating to others?
2. Why is it important not to share publicly about the problem you have with someone?
3. If there is a broken relationship in your world, what will you do about it? (Personal)

Chapter 7 – The Pressure Cooker

1. What do you consider to be the greatest stress in your life right now? Have you ever been burglarized or had a gun in your face?
2. What coping mechanism do you most often use to 'de-stress' yourself?
3. What in this chapter has helped you most to face and deal with your pressures?

Chapter 8 – Disruptive Moments

1. What are some major "disruptive moments" you have experienced? How did you handle them?
2. Which of these minor disruptive moments is the hardest for you to deal with? A guest dropping by unexpectedly? A sick

family member? A bad hair day? Forgetting an appointment? (Add your own.)

3. Will you determine today that, with God's help, you will view your next disruptive moment as a Divine Interruption?

Chapter 9 – The Necessity of Prayer

1. How would you describe your prayer life? Do you have a lifestyle of prayer?
2. Why is prayer a necessity for the Christian woman?
3. Do you have a prayer partner? Are you a member of a prayer group?
4. Why is it so important to pray for your family?
5. Did this chapter motivate you to cultivate a lifestyle of prayer?

Chapter 10 – Praise the Lord, Anyway

1. Have you learned to praise the Lord, anyway?
2. How does praise take our gaze from our circumstances?
3. What choices do you need to make today that will enable you to be full of faith instead of being filled with fear?
4. What choices do you need to make today that will enable you to be filled with peace instead of panic?
5. In what situation do you need to choose to praise the Lord, anyway?

Chapter 11 – Do You Need a Rest?

1. How would your family describe you? Restless? A person at rest?
2. Would you like to share what is causing this restlessness?
3. Are you carrying a heavy burden today? Share your burden with someone who will pray for you.
4. Has this lesson helped you in any way?

Chapter 12 – The Reckoning

1. Which "members" of your body are causing you the most difficulty? Your feet? Your mouth? Your eyes? Your hands?
2. Do you better understand the meaning of Romans 6:11?
3. Why is it important to examine our own lives and deal individually with each sin we discover?
4. Explain what it means to you that *sin does not have dominion over you.*

Chapter 13 – A Divine Intervention

1. Why is total surrender a prerequisite for contentment?
2. How do you find God's will for *your* life?
3. Today do you need to surrender to God: "Whatever, Whenever, and Wherever You want me to go and do?" (Personal)

Chapter 14 – The Satisfied Woman

1. Are you a "satisfied" woman? (Personal)

2. If not, can you pinpoint the areas in which you are not satisfied? (Personal)

3. What do you need to do to change your state of mind – your mindset? (Personal)

4. Can you affirm today that you are "learning to be content in the state in which you are?" If not, will you ask God to help you start that process?

5. Which part of this book was most meaningful to you? Which part was the most helpful? Were there any ideas that were new to you?

End Notes

Preface:

1   Philippians 4: 11b, *Letters to Young Churches,* A Translation of the New Testament Epistles, J.B. Phillips, New York, The MacMillan Company, 1958, page, 118.

2   *The Woman's Study Bible,* Dorothy Patterson, General Editor, Rhonda Kelley, Managing Editor, Holman Bible Publishers, Nashville, TN, 2014, page 2067. Used by Permission.

Chapter 1:

1   *Mother Wise,* Denise Glenn, Kardo International Publishers, 2009.

2   Philippians 4: 11b, KJV

3   Philippians 2:13, *Letters to Young Churches,* A Translation of the New Testament Epistles, J.B. Phillips, New York, The MacMillan Company, 1958, page 114.

4   Philippians 4: 11b NKJV

5   Author Unknown

Chapter 2:

1   Northwoods Inspirations LLC, 5530 West US HWY 2, Hurley, Wisconsin. Online Website.

2   Ibid.

3   Ibid.

Chapter 3:

1 *Experiencing God* Workbook, Henry Blackaby, Richard Blackaby, Claude King, LifeWay Press, Nashville, TN, 2007, page 69. Reprinted and Used by Permission.
2 *Joy of Living Bible Studies, Inc.*, Oak View California, 1986
3 James Dobson, *When God Doesn't Make Sense*, Tyndale House Publishers, Wheaton, IL, 1993, page 49. Used by Permission.
4 "Beyond the Shadow," Francis A. McDaniel. Used by Permission.

Chapter 4:

1 "Five D's of Satan's Strategy," Gladys Hunt, Tyndale House Publishers, Wheaton, IL. Used by Permission.
2 "He Giveth More Grace," Annie Johnson Flint, Copyright, 1942. In the Public Domain.
3 Author Unknown

Chapter 5:

1 *Five Things I Did Right and Five Things I Did Wrong in Raising our Children*, Sarah Maddox, Broadman and Holman Publishers, Nashville, TN, 2004, page 125.
2 *Lord, Let Me Love*, "God, Rescue Me From the If Onlies," Marjorie Holmes, Garden City, NY: Doubleday and Company, Inc., 1978, page 194.
3 *Five Things I Did Right and Five Things I Did Wrong in Raising our Children*, page 125.
4 Taken from *My Utmost for His Highest* by Oswald Chambers, edited by James Reimann, 1992, by Oswald Chambers Publications Assn., Ltd., and used by permission of Discovery House, Grand Rapids, MI 49501. All rights reserved, February 18 Devotional.
5 Ibid., February 18.
6 Philippians 3: 13
7 Op. cit., February 18

Chapter 6:

1   "Expectations," Frances McDaniel. Used by permission.
2   *You'll Get Through This*, Max Lucado, Thomas Nelson, Inc., Nashville, TN, 2013, page 89
3   Quote, Frances McDaniel.

Chapter 7:

1   *Awake My Heart*, "Daily Devotional Studies for the Year," J.Sidlow Baxter, Kriegel Publications, Grand Rapids, MI, 1960, 1994, page 39.
2   Matthew 5: 10
3   I Peter 2: 23
4   *Everyday Light*, Selwyn Hughes, Distributed by Broadman and Holman Publishers, Nashville, TN.
5   Used by Permission of P.M. (Name withheld.)
6   Colossians 1: 9-11

Chapter 8:

1   *When God Doesn't Make Sense*, Dr. James Dobson, Tyndale House Publishers, Wheaton, IL. 1993. Used by Permission.
2   Taken from "An Unforgettable Dinner on the Ground," by Charles R. Swindoll. Copyright 2010, by Charles R. Swindoll, Inc. All rights reserved. Used by Permission.
3   "His Purposed Plan," Frances A. McDaniel. Used by Permission

Chapter 9:

1   *Disciple's Prayer Life*, "Walking in Fellowship with God," T.W. Hunt, Catherine Walker, LifeWay Christian Resources, 1997.
2   *Experiencing God Workbook*, Henry Blackaby, Richard Blackaby, and Claude King, LifeWay Press, Nashville, TN, 2007, page 121. Reprinted and Used by Permission.
3   *Prayer*, O. Hallesby, Translated by Clarence J. Carlson, Augsburg Publishing House, Minneapolis, Minnesota, 1931. Forty-fourth Edition, 1953, pages 12-13.
4   *A Mother's Garden of Prayer*, Sarah Maddox and Patti Webb, Broadman and Holman Publishers, Nashville, Tennessee, 1999.

Chapter 10:

1 *You'll Get Through This*, Max Lucado, Thomas Nelson, Inc., Nashville, TN, 2013, page 89.
2 Francis A. McDaniel
3 *Praise the Lord, Anyway*, Francis Gardner Hunter, 1972.
4 II Chronicles 20
5 Ibid.
6 Ibid.
7 "Count Your Blessings," Words by Johnson Oatman, Jr., Music by Edwin O. Excell, *Baptist Hymnal*, page 585, LifeWay Worship, Nashville, TN, 2008
8 *You'll Get Through This*, Max Lucado, Thomas Nelson, Inc., Nashville, TN, 2013, page 89

Chapter 11:

1 *Vine's Expository Dictionary of New Testament Words*, Unabridged Edition, W.E. Vine, M.A., Macdonald Publishing Co., McLean, VA, page 969.
2 *The Random House Dictionary, Dictionary of the English Language*, Random House, Inc., New York, NY, 1966, page 1222.
3 *The Gospel of Matthew, Vol. II, Revised Edition, The Daily Bible Study Series*, Translated by William Barclay, The Westminster Press, Philadelphia, PA., 1975, pages 17-18.
4 *The Indwelling Life of Christ*, Major W. Ian Thomas, "How He Gives Me Rest," Multinomah Books, Colorado Springs, Co., 2006, pages 95-97
5 Ibid., Page 96
6 Ibid., Page 98

Chapter 12:

1 Dr. Cal Guy, Bellevue Baptist Church, Memphis, TN.
2 *Be Complete*, Warren Wiersbe, Victor Books, Wheaton, IL, 1982, pages 65-66.
3 Philippians 4: 11b-13, *Letters to Young Churches,* A Translation of the New Testament Epistles, J.B. Phillips, New York, The MacMillan Company, 1958.
4 *The Indwelling Life of Christ*, Major W. Ian Thomas, "A Question of Parentage," Multinomah Books, Colorado Springs, Co., 2006, page 41.

Chapter 13:

1   *Experiencing God Workbook*, Henry Blackaby, Richard Blackaby, Claude King, LifeWay Press, Nashville, Tennessee, 2007, page 21. Reprinted and Used by Permission.

2   Ibid. page 27

3   Ibid. page 27

4   Ibid. page 34

5   Ibid, page 47

6   *31 Days of Praise*, Ruth and Warren Myers, Multinomah Books, Colorado Springs, Co., 1994, page 78.

Chapter 14:

1   L. Jane Moline, *A Woman of Excellence*, from *A Woman's Garden of Prayer*, "A Perennial Challenge," Sarah Maddox and Patti Webb, Broadman and Holman Publishers, Nashville, TN, page 28.

2   *The Random House Dictionary, Dictionary of the English Language*, Random House, Inc., New York, NY, 1966, page 1222.

3   *Woman's Study Bible*, Dorothy Patterson, General Editor, Rhonda Kelley, Managing Editor, Holman Bible Publishers, Nashville, TN, 2014, page 2067. Used by Permission.

4   Ibid.

5   "He is Here," L. Kirk Talley, Kirk Talley Music, 1988. Used by Permission.

6   Op. cit. *Woman's Study Bible*

7   "Four Spiritual Laws," Bill Bright, Campus Crusade for Christ, Inc., 1965.

Appendix

WHAT TO DO WHILE WAITING
FOR GOD'S ANSWERS

A. GIVE GOD TIME

Psalm 27:14 (NKJV) *"Wait on the LORD, Be of good courage, And He shall strengthen your heart; Wait, I say, on the LORD!"* (See Psalm 37: 7, Psalm 130: 5-6, Isaiah 30:18)

B. PRAY WITHOUT CEASING

Luke 18: 1: *"....men ought always to pray and not lose heart."* James 5: 16 (NIV): *"The prayer of a righteous man [woman] is powerful and effective."* (See Jeremiah 33: 3, Philippians 4:6-7)

C. *STUDY GOD'S WORD*

II Timothy 3: 16-17, The New Living Translation reads: "All Scripture is inspired by God and is useful to teach us what is true and to make us realize what is wrong in our lives. It straightens us out and teaches us to do what is right. It is God's way of preparing us in every way, fully equipped for every good thing God wants us to do."

(See Psalm 119: 11, 105, Hebrews 4: 12)

D. CLAIM GOD'S PROMISES

I Peter 1: 2-4a (NKJV): *"Grace and peace be multiplied to you in the knowledge of our God and of Jesus, our Lord, as His divine power has given to us all things that pertain to life and godliness, through the knowledge of Him who called us by glory and virtue, by which have been given to us exceedingly great and precious promises…."*

(See Psalm 32: 8, Isaiah 26: 3, Isaiah 40: 28-31, Isaiah 41: 9-10, Hebrews 13: 5b-6, James 4: 8)

E. TRUST AND OBEY

If I am to live a life of contentment and victory, I must trust in the Lord and obey His commands.

Proverbs 3: 5-6 (NKJV): *"Trust in the Lord with all your heart, and lean not on your own understanding; in all your ways acknowledge Him, and He shall direct your paths."*

I John 5:3: *"For this is the love of God, that we keep His commandments. And His commandments are not burdensome"* (NKJV).

Psalm 18:30: *"As for God, His way is perfect; The word of the Lord is proven; He is a shield to all who trust in Him"* (NKJV).

Psalm 41: 10: *"Fear not, for I am with you; Be not dismayed, for I am your God. I will strengthen you, Yes, I will help you. I will uphold you with My righteous right hand"* (NKJV).

Psalm 32: 8: "I *will instruct you and teach you in the way you should go; I will guide you with My eye*" (NKJV).

(See Psalm 28:7, Psalm 40:4, Psalm 62: 10)

Micah 7:7: "*Therefore I will look to the LORD; I will wait for the God of my salvation. My God will hear me*" (NKJV).

About the Author

Contact Information for Sarah O. Maddox:
Email address: sarah.maddox@somrm.com

Published Books:

- *A Mother's Garden of Prayer*, co-authored with Patti F. Webb.

  Praying Scriptures for your children and grandchildren *from the womb to the tomb*. "Retreat daily to your own personal garden of prayer to intercede for the precious ones entrusted to you." (From the back cover.)

Available in hard cover and as an e-book at Amazon.com.

- *A Mother's Garden of Prayer Journal*, co-authored with Patti F. Webb (Not available).
- *A Woman's Garden of Prayer*, co-authored with Patti F. Webb.

  You can "discover a sacred, private place of walking and talking with the Lord daily" in this beautifully illustrated gift book that carries out the garden theme through Scriptures, stories and garden tips."

Available in hard cover and as an e-book at Amazon.com.

- *A Woman's Garden of Prayer Journal* (Not available).
- *Five Things I Did Right and Five Things I Did Wrong in Raising Our Children* by Sarah O. Maddox.

Mrs. Maddox was often asked the question, "If you could go back in time, how would you raise your children differently?" With transparency and openness, this Christian mother of two shares some of the valuable lessons she learned in her days of child rearing.

Available at LifeWay Stores and at websites on line.

- *A Beautiful Reflection* by Sarah O. Maddox

A Christian Novella based on Proverbs 27: 19: "As the water reflects the face, so the heart reflects the person." It is written to encourage young women of today to stand for their convictions and Christian beliefs in the face of an unfriendly culture.

Print book and e-book available at Amazon.com.